TWENTIETH-CENTURY PROFILES

Portraits from the French Press

An Anthology

xxpedient

Published by xxpedient

La Belle Étoile
19290
Chavanac
France

Published in 2013

Printed in Great Britain by Digital Print Media Ltd, St Ives

ISBN 978-2-9547111-0-2

Contents

Introduction

Gleaned from the French press, here are twenty-one portraits, frequently taking the form of obituaries. With the exception, beyond his own country, of Mgr Lustiger, the names are well known. The period in which they were made was 1940-89, with World War, followed by Cold War serving as reference points. These are largely 'Big Men', as well as one Iron Lady (not a representative ratio, but more than capable of holding her own). There are innovators, such as the photographer Henri Cartier-Bresson, although there is no Steve Jobs.

Nostalgia?

Beyond the pleasure of revisiting the familiar (but also the not so familiar: Georges Pompidou, Golda Meïr), the distinctive flavour offered by this collection is its provenance. This is partly a matter of being about France. To read the three presidents' obituaries – lives – together allows one to discover, in a pleasingly non-didactic fashion, how the unusual constitution originally crafted by and for General de Gaulle was bedded in. The fundamental nature of Mitterrand's opposition to the General is laid bare. It is nothing less than the question of legitimacy. The personal history of Pompidou, comparative dark horse, is told in detail, taking in his association with de Gaulle and the events of May 1968. Here, one can discover how Pompidou, Lustiger and their *bête noire*, Raymond Aron understood or reacted to *les événements*.

But, once dealt with in 'Part One – France', the collection is not so much about as from that country; it is the French slant that reveals Meïr and this group of famous men distinctively for English language readers. 'Part Two – Paris and Elsewhere' is shared by three natives, a visiting American ('Allow me to introduce myself: I'm the guy Jacqueline Kennedy has brought with her to Paris'), a German whose work destined him to live there, and an Iranian whose sojourn is explained by politics. Following that, the voyage is international, to 'East Europe and Beyond' (Part Three) then back to 'West Europe' (Part Four), concluding with its first subject's – Charles de Gaulle's – assessment of Winston Churchill. Whilst they make a, bookending, pair there are others that naturally suggest themselves, such as Sartre and Aron; Doisneau and Cartier-Bresson; Juan Antonio Samaranch and Giovanni Agnelli or, as studies in contrast, Mgr Lustiger and Ayatollah Khomeini; Meïr and Arafat.

A good example of the French style is provided by the title, *The Electrician who became President*: the bull taken by the horns, rather than being handled like fine bone china, as was the case with a 1992 BBC documentary, where it was hard to tell whether the discrepancy between President Walesa's one-time eating arrangements and the preparations for a Windsor Castle state dinner in his honour – place settings checked with a measuring rod – was being discreetly passed over or inferred. A difference of attitude towards power, probably. Whilst *L'État*, French or foreign, is not to be deprecated, nor is it to be deferred to. These portraits of heads of state and others are consequently lent not just historical but human interest, too.

Sakharov's fleeting parliamentary confrontation with Gorbachev reveals something callow about the latter: 'To one side, symbolising the opposition, an old man of controlled but unshakeable zeal, to the other, the man of power, in a sudden outburst of angry, disdainful authoritarianism.'

The 'anti-charismatic' and unloved chess player Karpov is imparted interest by the writer's recognition both of a trace of irony and that, 'possessed of an unblemished style, the world champion for ten years cannot be a total wretch'.

The possibility of a liaison between the future Jackie Kennedy and Agnelli is raised and gallantly dismissed: 'I may occasionally talk to ladies but never about them.' Actually, *Il Avoccato*'s portrait is one of the longest in the anthology, but sometimes there is no harm in lingering over glamour, when allied to achievement.

Field Marshal Montgomery puts in an unexpected appearance in the Karl Lagerfeld piece, 'wearing a superb duffle coat'; Mgr Lustiger meanwhile is seen in a soutane, speeding around the Quartier latin on his scooter. His 'Religious Leader' pairing, Ayatollah Khomeini, resembles 'something out of El Greco: a spade-like white beard and mystic's penetrating regard, beneath bushy black eyebrows and a turban the same colour'. Ho Chi Minh appears less forbidding. Nevertheless, 'the man … creates an immediate impression that will not be forgotten, by his very rare, burning look beneath bushy eyebrows, expansive brow and his sparser hair, a thing of spiky tufts. He would look a little comic, were it not for the dignity imbuing his profile and face'.

The French attitude to Third World leaders may be a residue of French colonialism, in which the transfer of its cultural values made for greater intimacy – the most obvious example being intermarriage – than the British Empire's administrative achievements. Ho Chi Minh and Yasser Arafat are sympathetically represented as leaders of their national struggles; the Ayatollah, just up to the point where he betrays the enlightened principles he had once espoused and, instead, gives revolutionary tribunals a free hand in meting out their summary justice.

A variety of styles is to be found here. When Tito died, his obituary ran to three, fact-filled, pages. The Marshal's was a prominent example of a long twentieth-century life. It comprised several acts, that were afforded by two world wars and various stages of the ideological/national struggle. On the other hand, the facts of Churchill's career probably did not need to be rehearsed for the portrait's original, French, readership. Instead they, and now we, are offered the thread of his life, fleshed out with ample quotation that is more – 'we are all worms, but I do believe that I am a glow-worm' – or less well known; for example his description of 'one of the darkest periods of my life' (after the Dardanelles disaster and dismissal from the Admiralty). 'Like a sea-beast fished up from the depths, or a diver too suddenly hoisted, my veins threatened to burst upon the fall in pressure.' There is the poignant moment when Eisenhower visited him in hospital towards the end: 'He just had the strength to hold out a trembling hand and place it in that of his brother-in-arms. According to witnesses, neither man spoke as they remained like this for several minutes.'

Further still from the detail of Tito's obituary is that which marked de Gaulle's passing. What is conveyed are rather the various stages of the statesman's relationship with the French people, from 18 June 1940 to 1969. More notes are on hand than is normal in the anthology, to clarify one or two areas of an impressionistic portrait.

Finally, the circumstances of an obituary may account for its tone. Tito's and de Gaulle's were, in the natural course of events, prepared. On 22 November 1963 the writer of *A Man of Goodwill* was in a state of shock. People, proverbially, remembered where it was they heard the news that day.

President Kennedy's assassination was the equivalent of 9/11.

R.P.
Suffolk, 2013.

Charles de Gaulle

The History Maker

'General de Gaulle is dead,' the five-column headline of 11 November 1970 announced. The obituarist was already the author of one, succinct biographical work. Although not a Gaullist, if anything aligning himself with the Opposition, his fascination for this extraordinary personality was to grow. Years later came a monumental life of de Gaulle.

(1970)

Besides Paul Reynaud and a coterie of political insiders, Marshal Pétain and a few hundred other soldiers, Daniel-Rops and an assortment of writers and journalists, who at the time knew the man who daringly presented himself in London?[1] [2] Who would have appreciated that the lofty silhouette at the back of the ministerial group making its way down the Élysée steps on 5 June 1940, wearing white gloves and a morose expression, and burning with indignation, if his eyes were to be believed, merited their attention? How many witnessed – fewer still one imagines – the sarcastic but fully involved presence which, from one château to the next, added itself to the roving and despairing war council; this man with a put-out demeanour who would soon emerge as the unashamed protagonist, instantly recognised as 'The Man of Destiny' by Churchill?

With sufficient curiosity and a necessarily clandestine approach it would have been possible, after a certain number of conversations and research of the written material, to piece together that: he had been Philippe Pétain's proud though deferential aide-de-camp; a number of his books had been published, advancing his case and revealing a familiarity with both Tacitus and Vauvenargues; at Metz, conspicuous in his white gloves, he had commanded a tank regiment and run up against a military commander by the name of Giraud; throughout the course of his career, from Warsaw to Trèves, at Beirut War College, from Great War imprisonment in Ingolstadt camp to the General Staff of the Fifth Army, he was recalled by those who had encountered him as a difficult, fascinating character, of superior calibre and with a superior still tone; his originality and proven courage were further reasons why those who had got to know him predicted a brilliant future, not without sometimes being driven to wish him ill.[34]

So it would be false to present the lone apparition in London as a miracle conjured up by blind chance. Although the path that led him there may seem obscure, the clarity of his conviction was long-standing. Now that the crisis had arrived, it was an event that his personality had been attending, however confusedly: he was ready to answer this call to the highest responsibility.

His claim, as an acting brigadier-general, to carry vestiges of French legitimacy with him was a pretty thin one but, within a matter of weeks, the London exile grew in stature and found his particular style. It was precisely his manner which succeeded in getting both Churchill and cross-Channel emissaries of the Resistance to take him seriously: an authoritative and never flagging intransigence; a discipline that would not infrequently come to be judged as inhuman. Gone was Pétain's sociable aide-de-camp, the attractive officer personality frequenting Beirut's salons, and the uninhibited participant who made his mark within Daniel-Rops' intellectual circle. Out of his bristling belligerence, principled stands and intransigence came instead a distance, that could be either sublime or intolerable. When they came to meet the man in whose name they were risking their lives, not even Resistance fighters were spared his hard-bitten humour. A secret agent taking his leave before returning to the continent was offered this cold comfort by his leader: 'In your line of work you are never going to be far from an unpleasant, messy situation.'

A *provocateur*'s plaudits

Provocation was a form of praise with him. He was most relaxed at the prospect of a decisive encounter, when his reflexes were at their most poised and his discernment most finely adjusted. It was at Mers-el-Kébir that Churchill became convinced that this difficult guest was, however wilful he could be, the one London-based ally whom he could communicate with as an equal, and the only Frenchman capable of overseeing his country's renaissance.[5] Here was someone who, like himself, saw the world not through the detail of a particular theatre's map but on its own, global, scale. There were times when the two men tussled; more often they stood shoulder to shoulder, allowing de Gaulle to manoeuvre France into the victor's camp.

By and by, in an almost paradoxical manner, the General's appeal was made known within his own camp, via paeans that took the form of polemics; an informal *mot juste* offered at some investiture; his distant expression, manifesting in photos pasted on the walls of legations dotted around the French territories. By a cumulative effect the appeal achieved its critical depth and intensity.

Finally the day arrived when an evacuee from a lost country, whose voice and legend were now known, set foot in his homeland once more, at Courseulles beach in the early morning of 14 June 1944. Would he be recognised by the French people, as the Dauphin had recognised Joan of Arc? The melancholy setting for these encounters between an astonished people and the man of 18 June were villages heavily marked by machine-gun fire.[6] The two parties took cautious stock of one another. De Gaulle, who had yet to attain a champion's aura with which to surf across a crowd's popular acclaim, proceeded uncertainly. He cut a rather disconcerting figure: the kids, *curés* and coppers from Bayeux to Isigny initially found much that was unusual about this face topping a lanky frame; the way he carried himself; his look. But as his name was conveyed by word of mouth, a crowd would gradually form, its circumspect surprise developing into attention and then a still warmer reception. It could now associate the nocturnal broadcasts' sharp voice – that of a demanding national prosecutor – with this outsized man, moving ponderously forward, in a camouflage pea-jacket.

Paris' encounter with the man who had gainsaid defeat came nine weeks later. Its first impression was of a uniformed Richelieu snuffing out *frondes* as they threatened in the street; a strict disciplinarian upholding order and the State, when revolution may have been equally likely.[7] Once de Gaulle had negotiated his way past these initial disturbances, he felt primed for August 26th's reciprocal communion with the crowd. As in

Normandy, his appearance struck the people from the Arc de Triomphe to Notre-Dame as perhaps unusual: his great height first of all, then his pallor; the lick of dark hair that stuck to his forehead, and the rather attractive maladroitness with which his long arms flapped back and forth. To begin with, his air of solitude stood out amidst the jostling liberty of the crowd. Then his appearance was outstripped by the determined desire that, theorising of the need for distance and mystery apart, he be 'familiar and fraternal'. De Gaulle made a noble way through the put-upon people but his presence, signifying the end of their captivity, was without condescension.

Once civil power had been vested in him, the General withheld himself from the populace another time. Power came naturally to this upstanding man, who did not shrink from the rigorous service that duty to the State commanded. Before, it was the enemy, defeatism and allies who remained, at best, dubious, to whom he had opposed his person, speaking with highly conscious and unerring deliberation. France's liberation in 1944 had depended upon this combination. Now it was the turn of the people who, acclaiming him, had brought the General to power, as well as the world beyond, to feel the force of his personality. His political experience was greater than might have been expected. This was one example of his talents' broadening; another was his astonishing authority, for whose assertion he never seemed to lack a pretext. He rejected any dilution or deviation from it, whether this took the form of a Liberation committee's failure to invoke the State, a minister acting without prior consultation, or of one of the Provisional Government parties' spokesmen venturing to criticise him. De Gaulle's bearing would then be cold and stormy. His resignation and withdrawal from the political domain came without warning on 20 January 1946.

Vercingétorix-cum-Caesar

At Colombey, the writing of his memoirs, an autobiography in the line of Vercingétorix, as though re-written by Caesar, was punctuated less by visits from an ungrateful French people – other than the RPF – than with solitary parkland walks in which he nursed his bitter reveries.[8][9] As well as walking, he read, smoked and occasionally travelled. His silhouette thickened, finally resembling a church prelate's. From time to time guests were invited; nevertheless he still had plenty of time to look out of his tower window onto a landscape taking its identity from the course of French history: Clairvaux, the Catalaunian Plains. Contemporary France was not just at the mercy of its rival factions and the militant left's 'separatists' but of America's dominant influence, and administrators who were preparing for a functionalist Europe. He was not sure her people were worth his attention. The 18 June call to arms and their shared resistance now lay in the past. History could assess him and his statue be erected in due course; for now he was Charles the private citizen.

De Gaulle would intermittently call a press conference – as for his 1955 adieus. For these occasions the mocking and sagacious prophet developed a kind of sardonic banter, during the course of which punishments on the one hand, and amnesties on the other, were handed out; some were marked out for oblivion, while others were granted access into the historical record. Those who conceived Europe as a polity were put on notice, whilst the Indochina peace treaty received his blessing; Sultan Mohammed V of Morocco was to be reinvested.[10] Curiosity concerning the great dispenser of contrasting fates was maintained, even after he made his way, mumbling anathemas and benedictions, back to his village.

Like a calcified block taking up station in his Voltaire chair he listened, with eyes half-shut and fair, ladylike hands resting upon his prelate's stomach, to those who, during the course of 1958, had travelled from Paris and Algeria to appeal to him: former prime ministers and National Assembly presidents, generals and partisans.[11] He knew both how to deflate the dangerous vacuum of power that existed and how to have power offered in the correct way by supplicatory legalists, before condescending to accept it.

Resident at the Élysée, it was noted how he was more civil even than the amiable M Coty.[12] In the Chamber a natural formal manner, combined with his ironic assurance, worked in putting the deputies at ease; they were not particularly perturbed when an occasional refined insolence made its way through all this politeness. He was still merely governing, although one could also date what might be called his reign, not from his inauguration in January 1959 but 15 June 1958 when, for the first time, de Gaulle appeared on the TV screen. The start of his second was not so unlike his original career's beginning. Then, it was the words he had pronounced via radio from London's Broadcasting House that had marked his historical arrival on 18 June 1940; now it was his apparition on the TV sets of ten million of his countrymen that alerted them to his return. Having insistently incited the menace, he had arrived just in time to avert a civil war.

A different type of connection was in the process of being formed. This unusual form of direct democracy passed 'from yourselves to myself'. It rested upon the masses' allegiance, that was too chalorous perhaps to be guaranteed, but which remained durable, thanks to the old man's feel for the new medium. Still inflexible, he nevertheless knew how to make his frequent talks both inspiring and touching.

The former prophet without a face, directing an 'Army of Shadows', had metamorphosed into a venerable gentleman who employed a rather studied courtesy and deliberately heavy irony as he helped himself to the plot of land named France, rather as if it was an unclaimed inheritance.[13] Where before his voice had sounded doleful and solemn, it could now be raised to a high but emphatic register that helped him impress himself upon the 'little people' leading their 'ordinary lives', as the successful man of destiny.

It did not take long for the TV screen to become a preferred tool of governance, more reliable even than the bank of foreign invitees who at Élysée 'press conferences' attested to his universal status, lest the French doubted it. On television certain physical features of de Gaulle became more evident. His eyes revealed, in the manner of an elephant's, resourceful cunning and cold rancour, both equally profound. His physiognomy, which age was no longer hollowing out to leave colourless creases as it once had, but was instead smoothing off like the weather's action on a mountain's summit, had a pink hue and, rounded out, conveyed a paternal sentiment, still kept in tension by the man's instinct for invective. Finally, the television set served to emphasise his forearms, whose loose articulation might, by a stretch of the military imagination, be compared to the tanks he had thrown onto the offensive on Abbeville's slopes, or of a sword defiantly lobbed at Caesar's feet. Useful in bringing a crowd to life, they seemed to have an independent function that helped him to reach out to the nation, its small platoons, its bedrock, as he undertook the State's defence against all that was foreign or opposed to it.

The focus of cameras and onlookers, and a nation by turns cast under his spell then put out by him, the Great Magician practised the alchemy he knew best: developing simple facts into a more coherent order and converting events into the themes which he wished to propose. The bank from which this wizardry principally drew was that of his own past and achievements. The General's vision, aided by the scale of his talent and ambition, his cheek even, was able, both then and now, to pierce into and change the course of history. Having such an intimate knowledge of the past, he knew how to mould it into a form that accorded with his destiny, which was itself sufficiently within his control to be adapted to an organic estimate of what the public interest demanded. This interest could be identified with a guiding leader who stood in the place of an otherwise disparate nation.

Then, from December 1965 the miracle of his ideas' transubstantiation no longer worked: harassed by a contrary, insolent movement of public opinion, the master hypnotiser's favourite charms now failed to convince.[14] This was the moment when one saw him change, with astounding opportunism, the register of his playing.

Much as the defiant lone figure of London had been transformed on 2 June 1958 into a suave prime minister handling constitutional change, so the old king now descended his throne and turned from stern prophecies to take up the benign art of conversation instead. The hoary sovereign revealed that he had the common touch and spoke of 'poor Churchill' as though he were a brother-in-arms who had passed away too soon; the former rebel was now Uncle Charles, who could look over his shoulder at his long past and all of its work. When questioned on his health a few months earlier, his sally to a thousand-strong press conference had been: 'Do not worry, I will not forget to die.' This type of jest, generally accompanied by either bitterness or vanity, he managed to carry off with his characteristic hauteur and gall, an acknowledgement of historical traditions and disdain for apparent disaster. It is with difficulty that one pictures his mutable face, which the tragedy of war, then politics' comedy, came to identify with a quarter-century of history, finally at rest.

Charles de Gaulle was born in Lille (Nord) on 22 November 1890. He died on 9 November 1970 at Colombey-les-Deux-Églises (Haute-Marne).

Georges Pompidou

Against the Grain

On 2 April 1974 Georges Pompidou died, prematurely, in office. Twelve years before, when he was named prime minister, the whole of France had been taken unawares: the General's principal stalwart stepped forward from the shadows and into the spotlight; the exercise of power revealed his qualities. Then, in May 1968, came the break with and superseding of de Gaulle. His obituarist recalls the skill and cultural ease of a man who lived his life against the grain.

(1974)

26 August 1944. With Paris only recently liberated, de Gaulle presses down the Champs-Élysées on foot, from the Arc de Triomphe to the Place de la Concorde. Around him there is a lively, brilliant cohort of true heroes and ministers, honorary marshals and dignitaries, resistants of the first and eleventh hour. The presence of a vast crowd, maybe two million strong, hems in on the regal progress. They acclaim him, shouting out their gratitude in the same breath that they recognise their own deliverance and the hopes that come with it. One of them – a

single grain of sand – is a long distance away from the great man and the yelling, springing companions. He is a thirty-year-old teacher called Georges Pompidou, whose war has been spent in Paris, where he has held a post at the lycée Henri IV.

8 January 1959. Once more the Champs-Élysées; once more de Gaulle. This time he is in a car, flanked by motorcycle outriders in their starched white gauntlets and the Household Cavalry with their shining breastplates, in full republican regalia. For the final approach to the Étoile, and according to plan, a reticent looking old man falls in: René Coty, the last president of the IV Republic. Here de Gaulle leaves him, an ear of corn rejected and blown away by history. The Parisians' acclaim can now be tasted properly by himself, the president of the V Republic. Though, who is the man who, following a signal, gets into the presidential car beside him? Could it be the president of the new National Assembly, just elected, or of the Senate and, according to protocol, the first in line of succession? Or is it the minister of justice, who is to be named prime minister within a few hours? Actually, it is the General's private secretary who, until yesterday, had been running a well-known investment bank to which, following any change in the fortunes of Gaullism and the new regime he will immediately return. Georges Pompidou.

11 November 1970. Two evenings before, on Monday the 9th, just after 7 pm, like an oak struck by lightning, the great man fell. The next day, the 10th, his closest companions arrived and assembled. General Massu, Michel Debré and the others regarded, for what seemed like an eternity, the face of their late leader, motionless forever now. Tears were shed.

At the end of the day a telephone call is received: the president of the Republic will come the next day with the prime minister in the early afternoon, to present themselves before the mortal remains. As a consequence, following the orders of Mme de Gaulle and her son, the village carpenter comes straightaway with a simple coffin that will hold the General's corpse. From now on, no-one is to see his features. For ten minutes only, the second president of the Republic, Georges Pompidou, stands in front of the closed coffin that is covered by a black sheet embroidered with silver teardrops.

Career

He came from Auvergnat peasantry stock. One grandfather had been a head-servant before becoming a tenant-farmer; the other a village craftsman. His own parents were both teachers in the country. To look at the family album, almost a carbon copy of the old lithographed series of stereotypes, would be to encounter the kind of life, full of republican virtue, that in the III Republic was held up for pupils' edification.

Following a scholarship to the lycée in Albi, in his baccalaureat year he won the national Greek prize before following the preparatory courses, in literature at Toulouse and general studies at Louis-le-Grand, for higher education. To be specific, the goal he was now aiming for was the École normale supérieure and qualifications which would pave the way to top-level public service.

But the competition in Paris was tougher than in Albi or Toulouse: in 1931 he came seventeenth in the written part of the examination, thirty-fourth in the oral and so failed to be amongst the thirty-one entrants. The following year he passed with distinction: first in his papers, eighth this time in the oral exam: perhaps speaking was not his forté. He had, as he would still have following thirty years in the banking world and the Conseil d'État – the corridors of power – a certain way of speaking which revealed that, beneath a Parisian polish, his origins were in the South and really quite humble. For example, when he pronounced *une pomme* or *une rose* it was as if these words were tempered in a throaty forge. Added to which were his almost too sonorous diction, a certain formal orotundity and his penchant for wide-ranging quotation.

Other characteristics that were to stay with him emerged very early on. The attitude adopted at the École normale supérieure was of not taking one's studies too seriously, however much of a facade this may have been. So as a student he appeared to spend his time quite freely, out and about in Paris. He was a regular in various bistrots, attended the theatre – later admitting that he had been to see Pabst's *L'Opéra de Quat'sous* eight times – and was a great cinema-goer. To supplement his finances he would give private tuition, as well as taking time out from preparing for the *agrégation* to attend lectures himself at Sciences-Po.[1] All this he did in a spirit of cultured dilettantism that did not altogether hide the fact that he had moral reserves to call upon, which were allied to a sound judgement and well-honed reasoning. From his peasant ancestry he inherited solid common sense and a distrust of surface glitter; the habit of logical reasoning and respect for intellectual values he had from his teacher parents, both being cardinal virtues of the primary school. He had furthermore, and to the highest degree, three characteristics which, depending on the circumstances, could be viewed in a positive or negative light: stubbornness, cunning and prudence.

Once again, in the *agrégation*, he was first but without drawing any laudatory remarks from the examiners. Their chairman even went so far as to regret the result on account of its apparent ease. The formality of a year's military service having been distractedly complied with, first as an officer cadet at St-Maixent and then as a second lieutenant at Clermont-Ferrand, his career path was now clear: starting in the new, 1935, academic year, he took up a post at the St Charles lycée in Marseille as a teacher of letters and classics: French, Latin, Greek. He was twenty-four and, with his future settled, could now marry. Back in Paris, a friend from Louis-le-Grand, Léopold Senghor, introduced him to Claude Cahour, a tall blonde girl who had just begun her first year of law studies, the daughter of a doctor from Château-Gontier. Her amused curiosity, both in people and things, and the way she had, which could be either pacific or audacious, of taking life as it came, chimed with the young teacher's cultured casualness.

Marseille worked well in certain ways, but Paris' greater variety drew the unorthodox young couple, open to life. In October 1938 he secured a post at the lycée Henri IV. A little three-room apartment was found in the rue José-Maria-de-Heredia, close to the Invalides, from which, after the war, they would move to the rue Charlemagne, by the Marais, before arriving opposite Notre-Dame on the Île-de-France, at an address on the quai de Béthune, a move that their developed taste suggested and their finances would permit. For the moment they went out a great deal and met new friends. Life was easygoing and fun. When war came, his infantry service in the mountains was to be no more than a brief interlude, fitting neatly into the 1939-40 school year; afterwards the teacher returned to his pupils at 'Henri IV'. An adopted son, Alain, who is now a doctor with two children of his own, completed the family in 1942. Could one detect any political leanings then? While at the École normale supérieure he kept his distance from both the small band of Liberals, formed by the future IV Republic minister, René Billères, and a Left circle that revolved around Jacques Soustelle. His own family were socialist, with his father a steadfast party member who had known Jaurès and campaigned for Paul-Boncour.

As a Normalien in the Latin quarter, he did not hesitate to counter-demonstrate against Action Française's foot soldiers with the LAURS (Ligue d'action universitaire républicaine et socialiste – University Republican and Socialist League of Action), whose meetings he frequently attended and at whose rallies he occasionally spoke.[23] Nevertheless, he did so with an attitude of detached curiosity, nonchalance even. Having returned to Paris again in 1938, his leftist sympathies remained a private affair, nothing more. He had, one might say, 'ideas' rather than any firmly held convictions. Under the occupation, when he was preparing pupils destined for the colonial institute, he was quite open as to where his hopes and sympathies lay - with the Resistance. He did not though undertake any great risks and, above all, kept his distance, as he always would. Even when he became closely associated with Charles de Gaulle, he did not join his first party, the RPF, during the period 1947-52 and later only became a member of the UNR in 1962 – as prime minister.[45] At the top of the greasy pole he was often to be heard maintaining that it was by chance he found himself there, and not because he had intrigued and jostled and coveted getting to this point. Nobody was fooled, it almost goes without saying, realising that this kind of attainment could only be grasped by effort and strength. Weapons at Pompidou's disposal included cunning, derived from his Montboudif peasant ancestors; his pride, that was rooted in modesty, and the unyielding patience of the genuinely ambitious.

Confidant of the General

Autumn 1944, with everything else going on following the

Liberation, was not really the time to be pushing for a post, but there was no harm in reacquainting oneself with old friends who might be useful.

ENS contemporaries were dotted about in the various high-level posts they had since achieved: Jean-Paul de Dadelsen invited him to try the Ministry of Information, and Émile Laffont, now the Home Office private secretary, 'la préfectorale'.[6] Then René Brouillet, who had been charged with finding 'a qualified teacher who knows how to write', to act as a go-between with the Ministry of Education, picked him out. It was a very attractive offer, although it involved leaving the administrative for the political sphere, and security for the uncertainty of representing a provisional government that might quite possibly be short lived. Later Georges Pompidou would confide that the decision to leave the teaching profession had been the most difficult of his life.

Two months would pass before the representative received a summons from the man of destiny, although this too would turn out to be a non-meeting; it was a Saturday when he happened to be in the office; de Gaulle asked that 'someone should be sent for', without delay, to help settle a lively governmental difference of opinion. In the event, the cabinet meeting was chaired by Gaston Palewski, with the help of Louis Vallon, Étienne Burin des Roziers plus René Brouillet and his aides.

De Gaulle's resignation came as much as a surprise for Georges Pompidou as it did for the average man in the street, since he played too small a role within the cabinet to be told what was about to occur, or be a party to its collective testament.

He was assured that a job with the Conseil d'État was intended for him and, in the meantime, was placed at the Tourism Board. Here he introduced, in his lighthearted gourmet's fashion, Hôtels de Luxe, de Baumanières Hall at Baux-de-Provence being one of the first. He was also the guiding light behind exhibitions that would gain him his red sash. Amongst them was 'Eight centuries of British civilisation', inaugurated by the future Queen Elizabeth II and the Duke of Edinburgh.

The school year grew closer and he grew restless, turning over the advisability of a return to teaching. When September actually arrived, the decree naming him Conseil d'État counsel was signed. He took up his post within the litigation section, which managed to combine the hardest work with the least glamour. Throughout the eight years he spent at the Palais Royal he carried on a long complaint. But at the same time as he fulfilled his responsibilities there, which remained relatively unimportant, he took on others that were prestigious and secret. This was the start of his intimate association with General de Gaulle.

Almost immediately, he revealed an ability to sort out meddlesome, unavoidable problems that was of the highest order. His efficiency and discretion were guaranteed. Mme de Gaulle began to swear by 'Georges'. For his part, the General warmed to his dedicated services. He did not take long in forming the view that, apart from skill, this Pompidou possessed good sense and judgement, not to mention political nous. Unlike the rest within his orbit – the agitators – he did not clamour for a post, nor impose in other ways.

Before long he had become indispensable and, in 1948, de Gaulle installed him at the head of his kitchen cabinet, working with Jacques Foccart and Claude Mauriac, almost hidden from sight in the rue de l'Université, away from the RPF's public seat and centre of activity in the rue Solferino. Every day he would prepare a digest of the political situation. The others – Malraux,

Frey, Debré, Soustelle, Chaban-Delmas, Fouchet, Vallon, Palewski – could share the limelight of battle; outside the Conseil d'État, Sciences-Po, where he taught some courses, or the jury of the ENA, on which he sat, it was enough for him to be the General's man.[7]

Working this way for six years to 1954, a byword for discretion, his role remained known to only a few. His manner may have appeared carefree and almost pliable but, in reality, he had nerves of steel and, far from being absent-minded, was constantly on the alert, assessing and planning. Luck had been on his side perhaps, but he had made it that way. Stepping down simultaneously, at the beginning of 1954, from the Conseil d'État and de Gaulle's kitchen cabinet he did not step aside. The cabinet now consisted of just two adherents, Olivier Guichard and Colonel de Bonneval, whilst he was established as the closest and, more importantly still, most listened-to adviser.

The strategist's tactician

A year earlier, he had countered Jacques Soustelle, the RPF secretary-general's, argument for the movement to continue, and prevailed with his own strategy of withdrawal, so as to wait for a better day. At the same time it was he who organised the bidding between three publishers, Plon, Gallimard and Laffont, for the General's *Mémoires de Guerre*.

Then, in a further balancing act, the former school teacher who had become a junior representative and little known Conseil d'État counsel, and who had developed a certain stature, moved seamlessly to within the establishment, as a director of Rothschild Bank. This came about in a straightforward, apparently easy manner, like much of his career. Following the 1951 election campaign, an effective death knell for the RPF, it had been necessary to restore the Gaullist finances. So the head of the private cabinet had visited the bankers. One of them was René Fillon, a qualified languages teacher, who was now chief executive at the Rothschild family bank. There was a mutual rapport between them that prompted Guy de Rothschild to take Georges Pompidou on, knowing that – bored and with nothing more to gain from it – he was on the verge of quitting the Conseil d'État. The banker wanted to maintain links, through such a close associate as Pompidou, with the General. Not that he had a specific role to offer him; instead a waiting period, decked out with various roles and titles, suggested itself.

It was thanks to a long journey they made together not long after, across sub-Saharan Africa, laying the basis for *Cofimer*, an investment company, that the newcomer to the bank was able to put his many talents to use; the Baron was won over by his conjuring intuition and acuteness to human relations, plus his even, good-natured temperament, his interestingly lively conversation. In 1956 René Fillon was elected governor of Sudan and Georges Pompidou succeeded him as chief executive.

In spring 1958 Pompidou – with Algeria boiling over and excitement gaining amongst the Gaullists, who were in a confusion of cabals and in the expectation of arriving in power, the promised land – retained his sardonic distance. More than ever he was the General's, rather than Gaullism's, man. His thinking, perspectives and advice were all reserved for the former; the latter he regarded with playful irony, and he would pass the time of day with them indulging his relaxed and sceptical manner. Some, most notably Michel Debré, found it hard to stomach.

When he moved into the Hôtel Matignon, as principal private secretary, it was already well understood in political circles that he was Berthier to de Gaulle's Napoleon.[8] As André Malraux put it, 'the strategical visionary's nuts and bolts counterpart'. Only Napoleon never made Berthier his No.2.

During the second half of 1958, he was the conduit via which everything of significance passed. He alone had direct access, day and night, to the General, through the door that linked their two offices. At the same time as he remained unknown to the general public, for those who knew better he was the indispensable man.

This was how he came to be honoured by him, with evident symbolism, on the day de Gaulle arrived at the Élysée, 9 January 1959. The Champs-Élysées: fifteen years had elapsed since Georges Pompidou stood at the rear of the tumultuous crowd which had gathered to greet the liberator; this time, in recognition of ten years' steady work behind the scenes, followed by six months of total commitment to the cause, he stood at the side of the new regime's founder. But if he were strolling down the boulevard the following day he wouldn't draw a second glance from anyone. French people knew neither his face nor his name.

His perseverance had been rewarded; though this was not the time to jettison his astute, prudent approach. He turned down the chance to be Debré's minister of finance. When the six-month sabbatical he had taken from the bank was over, he simply resumed his duties in the rue Lafitte. He would not give them up, together with his chairman- and directorships, until 1962 to take up an official post – nothing less than the premiership. Without any particular fuss, he completed four years in the private sector with the official dignity of a member of the Constitutional Court, which included handing back to the Treasury the salary that normally went with this position. (...)

As early as 1960, when his friend Philippe de Croisset began to bitterly criticise Michel Debré, bringing de Gaulle into the equation too, he let him know that, as far as he was concerned it was best not to 'push the point too hard. Because when Debré is sacked or more likely resigns, I will be succeeding him as prime minister'. Croisset, scarcely believing what he was being told, but nevertheless impressed, subsequently kept silent. The whole thing was remarkable. Until his nomination as prime minister he continued as before: in February 1961 the task of secretly renewing talks with the Algerian rebels was confided to him: he had performed others. Throughout Sunday 23 April 1961, when the Generals' *putsch* in Algeria entered its second day, he was at de Gaulle's side: again, he had performed a similar role more than once before. Only days later he would decline the post of minister of finance for a second time, surely the right decision if he was liable to be offered, sooner rather than later, an even higher post.

The nomination of 16 April 1962 came as a surprise to everyone: political class, Gaullist movement, indeed the whole of France. Only a few of the country's most powerful insiders, together with a handful of alert 4th *arrondissement* party bosses, knew and understood. There had been a high price to pay in terms of both persistence and restraint but now the path he had trodden, slowly and patiently in the big man's shadow, had reached a clearing. Three separate careers were coming to an end and, in their place, a destiny was beginning.

Six decisive months

Immediately after the referendum, that gave an overwhelming and unequivocal 'Yes' to the ratification of the Algerian Peace Treaty, finally concluded in March 1962, Michel Debré advised a dissolution of Parliament and fresh elections. Instead of sending the deputies back to their constituencies de Gaulle chose to part company with his prime minister, hoping to broaden the base of his majority as an alternative to another campaign trail. (…)

There were to be four months when events constantly threatened Georges Pompidou with defeat in Parliament, or, left to his own devices by the ruler, to be swept away by the storm. Independence prompted chaos and violence in Algeria, where general panic followed the *pieds-noirs'* departure. Manoeuvring and splits, both within the Gaullist ranks and those of the Majority, became increasingly common. Gathering momentum in its passage across the country, a wave of social unrest unfolded. In August it seemed as if the prime minister might be able to regain his breath and glimpse a spot of calm, but then came a burst of machine-gun fire at Petit-Clamart: the attempted assassination.

To de Gaulle this was the sign for action. For a year he had warned that: 'From the moment peace is concluded they will try to eliminate me.' He was referring not to the killers waiting in ambush by the road but his old enemies, the political class, the parties. 'So I will attack,' he would say. After his miraculous escape from the fusillade this is what he did.

The chosen battle horse was to be an amendment of the constitution, allowing for presidential election to be by direct, universal suffrage. Losing his National Assembly majority, the confrontation's first victim was the head of government. For the first and the last – to 1974 – time under the V Republic, there was a clear ministerial crisis.

When Michel Debré asked him for a dissolution of Parliament in April 1962 de Gaulle's response had been to retain the National Assembly and to get a new prime minister instead. But on 5 October, when 280 of the 480 deputies voted against the government in a censure motion, it was to keep his prime minister and dissolve the Assembly.

The October referendum resulted in a positive, if ambiguous, decision: while the majority who voted were in favour, for the first time the 'Yes' vote represented less than half of those eligible to vote. The November elections, on the other hand, were a near triumph with the UNR obtaining 233 seats, around which its coalition could form an absolute majority in the Bourbon Palais. The prime minister was able to carry on in office; the six most critical months were over, both for him and for the French people.

The statesman emerges

The spectacle emerged, for those who followed public affairs, of a statesman being born, 'live' and in the spotlight. 'One can see him growing before one's eyes,' remarked François Mauriac during a TV appearance.

The pear-shaped, old-school radical-cum-leisurely-aesthete concealed a very strong character, whose insensitivity could be of grand proportions. Capable of switching in an instant from a jovial demeanour to being cuttingly dry, he could give off cold fury or absolutely refuse to give way. Dilettantishly vague though he may have seemed, in fact he was unrelenting at work. Even if he was able to penetrate very quickly to the essence of a brief, twelve hours' uninterrupted work was not a problem for him. Shortly, the model, almost self-effacing, right-hand man was displaying a confident authority. How he appeared to others — whether accommodating, brilliant or rigorously doctrinaire — did not matter much to him: it was more important, in each case, to be useful, effective, pragmatic. Not for a moment could he neglect the issue of the succession, and it was imperative that he should not, since it had so many ramifications. Whilst he could not make any preparations for this significant day and was even required to make a credible pretence that he was not interested by it, the issue would not go away for the No.2 to a hero who was now in his seventies and starting to tire.

On more than one occasion already, first the evening of 22 August 1962 and next when de Gaulle had to undergo heart surgery at Cochin Hospital on 17 April 1964, Georges Pompidou contemplated the imminence of the event, minute by minute. Then in spring 1965 the General appeared to hesitate as to whether he should seek a second mandate.

This was the year that the prime minister began to speak forcefully of the 'historical task' de Gaulle and now he had undertaken, 'an unprecedented project of national renovation', that called for 'the presence at the head of the State of a figure whose authority was strengthened by the people's confidence'. Pompidou had found a new voice. He had changed. He no longer felt obliged, as he had at the outset of his government, when the Council of Ministers met, to spend his whole time gauging the expression of his more august counterpart, so as to anticipate his thinking and responses, or to take upon himself the burden of everything that went wrong, whilst willingly allowing the president to take the credit for each success. The chance of being repudiated by, or having a row with, him did not fill him with dread now; nor was he frightened to criticise, including in public. He was sure of himself. He purred a little, it seemed. Though when he was contradicted or argued with, his claws came out to cause harm. François Mauriac called him 'The Little Wild Cat' and this description by the reign's Froissart – or Saint-Simon? – stuck.[9][10]

If he began to weary and irritate the prickly, suspicious old man, did Georges Pompidou realise it? Did he know that his own successor had already been chosen and advised to stand ready, and that Couve de Murville was only prevented from taking up residence at the Hôtel Matignon by not securing a seat in the March 1967 parliamentary election?

The fall from grace

The 1967 elections, third stage it was said of the 1965 presidential consultation, were a relative setback to the government, which now held only a one-seat majority over the Left. The opposition felt that the tide had turned in its favour whilst the Gaullists, if they had not lost the election itself, abandoned the illusion that their leader was invincible. Unfairly, he placed the blame for this worrying turn of events on his prime minister.

However, Pompidou did not appear unduly worried by the bad-humoured criticism. More at ease than ever, his priority was now to develop his own stature on the international scene, via a series of trips and high-level meetings, whilst leaving a relatively free hand at home to his minister of finance, Michel Debré. He was happy limiting himself to the occasional – and usually muscular – skirmish with the previous minister, M Giscard d'Estaing who, since his January 1966 sacking, had become a difficult partner, unhelpful in his frequent interventions. In general, the government now felt unchallenged and complacent, whilst the country was becoming bored, through the lack of either a challenge to contend with or of any common cause. It was the younger generation which grew restless and felt the urge to express itself.

The student revolt in May 1968 caught everyone, most significantly the General and his government, off guard. Its outset appeared so unthreatening that, leaving Paris on 2 May, Georges Pompidou went ahead with an official visit to Iran and Afghanistan. When he returned on the 11th the uprising, that met with a hardline response, was at its most intense.

Three hours after landing at Orly and having consulted with the General, the prime minister made a television appearance to announce various measures, which abandoned the hard line taken in his absence. Almost immediately it was clear that he, in contrast to the reaction of a sizeable part of the leadership when faced with the student revolt and the workers' strike that then, rather bizarrely, merged with it – disarray and nerviness culminating in a funk – had not lost his sang-froid or ability to maintain and use what power remained at his disposal. Levers appeared jammed and then not to work at all in response to a succession of events, whether violent, or simply dramatic or even burlesque. Nevertheless, in a country that appeared, piece by piece, to be coming apart, he tried to keep a grip on the situation. De Gaulle, who was both unconcerned and non-comprehending, said nothing. Encouraged by his prime minister, he left for Romania between 14-18 May, on a trip that had been organised a long while before. Georges Pompidou meanwhile stood up against parliamentary attacks, the turmoil at the barricades and the feeling of crisis that was spreading across the country, even if it seemed that as soon as he had staunched a breach here or snuffed out the flames there, elsewhere a flood or fire had developed.

Each man – again, so it seemed – had one final card to play. For the president, on 24 May, this was to call for a referendum on the proposal he was making for a more participatory, or regionalised, democracy. For the prime minister it was the opening, the following day, of round-table discussions, with the government as moderator, between business interests and unions. It soon became clear that, on the one hand the referendum was not to be the intended cure-all and would have to be abandoned while, on the other, the spokesmen of Grenelle may have reached an accord but the strikes had not come to an end. They would continue for several more weeks. The left opposition now roused itself, declaring that it was ready for the handover of power or, alternatively, to pick it up where it found it, seeing that the state was on the verge of collapse.

The king's secrets

The memory of how the tables were turned to produce the opposite outcome remains fresh: de Gaulle's disappearance on 29 May, followed by his return the following day. The address to the nation, then the announcement that the referendum was to be abandoned and Parliament dissolved. Finally, the reversal's culmination, and Gaullism's riposte to the Left's own mass march of 13 May, a vast cortège along the Champs-Élysées. The extent of the prime minister's involvement in the 'disappearance' was much debated: did he know about it from the start or was he warned just moments before it occurred? Was he a party to it? Georges Pompidou never spoke about this.

Leaving aside the detailed facts and subsequent conjecture, it is likely that, from his perspective, these forty-eight hours can be summarised as follows: the General, although he did not explicitly take his No.2 into his confidence, left enough clues that were sufficiently of a pattern for him to deduce that this kind of move was about to be made. He would have also known that the date of the big demonstration, whose 'green light' Gaullist leaders had been clamouring for, had been fixed, with the General's approval, for the Thursday afternoon, the 30th. He had tried since the 27th to persuade de Gaulle to both jettison the referendum and to proceed with the dissolution of Parliament.

It was only at the last minute however, as the Council of Ministers extraordinary meeting was due to start in the early afternoon of the 30th, that Pompidou gained acceptance of this last point; at the same moment he was told that his offer of resignation had been rejected: he would stay as head of government and the first task he was required to perform was to reshuffle the cabinet, moving those with ministerial responsibility away from the posts directly called into question by *les événements*. Georges Pompidou would later reveal how, from then on, his position was provisional, that he was in fact a condemned man: it was he who must bear full responsibility, seeing that his government had been in power for six years when 'May' arrived. Its increasingly dramatic events were attributed to the choices and decisions he had made. His insistence on holding elections would also be held against him, if these were lost.

But they resulted in a triumphant victory. The prime minister's decisiveness had taken over where presidential charisma left off, causing an impressive stir. Within ten days of the election, and after a convoluted sequence of events – his resignation tendered then withdrawn, not accepted then accepted – the brilliant dauphin and irreplaceable prime minister was shooed out of office, as though he had been guilty of betraying the elderly sovereign. But was this fatal? Proposing a toast to 'Monsieur le député du Cantal' at the meal marking his government's departure, André Malraux proclaimed: 'I drink to your destiny.' This talismanic word would soon be reiterated by Georges Pompidou on his own behalf. (...) Even today though, not all the ins and outs of this tense period have been explained.

Amongst them was the Markovic affair, so called because it

involved the death of a young Yugoslavian bodyguard working for Alain Delon, the actor.[11] The affair began with a rather louche news item that would be exploited – five years later it is still not known by whom – to try and undermine Pompidou. The concerted effect of scandalous gossip, tampered photos and documents, together with the wringing out of false testimonies, malevolent accusations and abuse of rights, gathered momentum. The air was thick with calumny. Without dwelling on either the complexities of the situation or the urgent attempts by his former No.2, both directly and by letter, to get the General involved, the dirt kept streaming on, without anything being done about it. One could sense that, at the back of it all, lay the desire to get rid of the heir presumptive.

So Georges Pompidou rebelled. In Rome in January 1969, and the following month on Swiss television, he declared that, when the General retired, he would be standing as a candidate for the Élysée; he spoke of the 'national role' he felt destined to play. The first announcement provoked a fury and withering response, out of all proportion with the cause. Following the second, the rupture was complete. No one any longer dared mention in front of de Gaulle the name of his previous long-term and most faithful and trusted lieutenant. On 27 February, when he was invited to address the directors of the Chamber of Commerce, Georges Pompidou's speech had the flavour of a detailed manifesto. Accusations of 'treason' echoed around the Élysée.

Then, on 4 March, the legal process of the Markovic affair recommenced and placed the former prime minister under the public spotlight once more. Refusing to accept that this might be a coincidence, he complained publicly to the General who, on this occasion, had to break his silence: the slight was too important and its orchestration too blatant to do otherwise.

Eight days later the General and Mme de Gaulle received the rule's two former prime ministers, Michel Debré and Georges Pompidou, for dinner at the Élysée, accompanied by their wives. It was a meal intended to repair the damage done, rather than to bring about any reconciliation.

Both guests wrote of this icy and tense, even sinister, evening, leaving no doubt that the affection, service and mutual respect of the past were well and truly dead. De Gaulle judged that he had been betrayed; Pompidou that he had been fed to the pack. The result was that this would be their last meeting. During his last twenty months the General would not encounter the man who, before ultimately succeeding him as head of state, had been so close for twenty years. Georges Pompidou would not see his chief's face again. When he came to Colombey to bow his head before the mortal remains, as described at the beginning of this piece, the family had made sure the coffin lid was closed. Shakespeare could not have written it better.

While this saga was being played out behind the scenes, the forefront of domestic affairs was occupied by preparations and campaigning for the referendum on decentralisation. Once again de Gaulle was making a personal appeal to the nation for his reinvestiture; for a blank cheque, in effect.

Without any alternatives on offer, the old conjuror might have his way again by, in effect, saying, as he had before, 'double or quits'; 'myself or chaos'; 'a "Yes" or I go'. But that was the point: this time there was an alternative; people either knew or felt that Georges Pompidou, with his competent, energetic reputation intact, had every chance of succeeding to power. It was also known, however, that the Gaullist dukes and barons were exerting all their influence to get an explicit, public commitment from the heir presumptive that, in the event of a 'No' vote, he would not stand. A sacrifice was required of him.

'Gaullism defeated, post-Gaullism cannot stand in its stead,' proclaimed André Malraux. 'Supposing a "No" vote,' *La Nation* wrote, 'it is evident that no Gaullist candidacy can be satisfactory.'

The vote was lost by a narrow margin. Pompidou performed his role in the campaign, but without any zeal or belief. He was now ready for office himself. Edgar Faure, Valéry Giscard d'Estaing and Jacques Duhamel had all been successfully canvassed and his future prime minister was already chosen. The 27 April 'No' result carried him to power. It was the end of an era. That which was replacing it, said André Malraux disparagingly, was going to be 'politics with a small "p" '.

Relatively more anonymous as president

As only he stood a chance of winning, Georges Pompidou was to be the unchallenged candidate of the Majority. The recipient of a bursary at Albi lycée, socialist student at the École normale supérieure, schoolteacher, and discreet adviser had completed his journey. After six years as the second in command, followed by eleven months consigned to the political wilderness, he was the French leader. But he was not yet the pre-eminent Frenchman.

In the seventeen months from his election to the death of General de Gaulle, the president of the Republic appeared restrained and relatively anonymous, as if he were intimidated. His initiatives were limited and his involvement in dealing with events even less so. News cameras focused less on the Élysée than on his prime minister, Jacques Chaban-Delmas at the Hôtel Matignon, where a ministry of all the talents generated programmes, practical policies and wide-ranging goals, the most striking being to create a 'New Society' aimed at improving the 'quality of life'.

There was one notable exception to the president's comparative reserve: the EEC Hague summit that was held on 1-2 December. Taking the lead, he made strong proposals that had a tonic effect on France's five partners, for both the undertaking of economic and monetary union and for the expansion of the Common Market, which Great Britain would join on 1 January 1973. This was by way of payment to the Independent Republicans and centrist 'Europeans', in exchange for their support.[12] At The Hague a new page in European history seemed to have been turned. (...)

With the death of his former chief, Georges Pompidou assumed his role centre stage, finally feeling his hands were not tied. He moved smoothly, decisively to assert his grip. The prime minister's and government's relinquishing of control was accentuated, as he made his wider-ranging authority and the primacy of the presidency clear. Very quickly, this change in attitude embittered the existing malaise between the regime's No.1 and No.2. An almost permanent, unstated conflict took hold between them. (...)

In 1971 'scandal' filled the news: a variety of unlawful money and property deals, compounded by others that were less than transparent, produced a bad smell. In actual fact, the accused individuals were only middle-ranking officials or members of the government. (...) The regime's aura was seriously damaged by these continual, saga-like, revelations. A further one came at the beginning of January 1972, when *Le Canard Enchainé* published details of the prime minister's tax return suggesting that, with skilful use of credits, he had managed to evade paying some of his contribution. Targeted by these allegations, M Chaban-Delmas was dangerously slow in reacting.

A personal diplomacy

Subsequently his fate was sealed. The president, having fully regained control of the levers of power, was now casting his mind forward to the parliamentary elections. As the landslide majority from June 1968 could not be maintained, various considerations had to be run through. Whether to call them early, ahead of the parliament's prorogation in spring 1973? Was the prime minister well enough equipped to organise and carry through the first election since the General's death? How could he put his prerogatives to best use, so as to give the Majority an early advantage? To find his way towards an initial answer to these questions, Pompidou decided to test public opinion itself. He chose to hold a referendum on the surprising subject of Great Britain's proposed entry into the EEC. There was something admirably skilful about this ploy to both divide the opposition between 'Europeans' and communists and to refashion an enlarged majority. If it came off then the parliamentary elections could be held against a backdrop of public enthusiasm, generated by the issue of 'Europe' and its production of new alliances and divisions.

A lacklustre, not very well conducted campaign failed to capture the public's interest. With nearly 40% abstaining and 7% of the ballot papers damaged, higher figures than for any previous referendum at national level, the French people had not so much said 'Yes to Pompidou' as shown their indifference to his consultation, his leadership, himself. This was the president's first significant setback.

After weeks of uncomfortable reflection, bordering on disillusion, Georges Pompidou made his mind up to take action in a counter-attack. Forced to assume responsibility for the failure of a tactic whose implementation he had simply complied with, his prime minister insisted that he be allowed to place a no-confidence motion before Parliament. He hoped that he would then be able to both reassert his authority there and let the country see that the referendum's ambiguous outcome had jeopardised neither the coalition nor his own position. Within political circles though it was understood that he was no longer part of the power equation: for example, the reform of the ORTF's (Office de radiodiffusion télévision française) rules of incorporation regime was planned and carried through without his involvement. After initially refusing to, Pompidou reluctantly allowed the motion to be proposed; on 23 May M Chaban-Delmas won the vote by 368 to 96. This did not prevent him being asked, six weeks later, to step down, which he did with a fairly bad grace. There was a flurried exchange of letters, in which his studied courtesy still left the scarred feelings caused by his rejection, coming so soon after the vote of confidence, plain to see. M Pierre Messmer, who succeeded him on 5 July, was a Gaullist of sterling qualities, cold, a man of integrity. He did not appear in front of Parliament until the summer recess ended in October. There seemed no need to him to seek a vote of confidence. Instead there was to be a return to the regime's Gaullist roots, evident in the choice of language and men, and the reawakening of myths.

In the country at large, meanwhile, people were protesting for the environment or liberalisation of the abortion laws, and against racism or the Larzac military base being enlarged, with greater fervour than either for or against the UDR and Left coalition. Revolt, that had seemed spent, now appeared to enjoy an occasional revival amongst the youth, especially college students.[13] But the president was himself unmoved by these movements: order, first and foremost, had to be maintained and that was that. Having, from the start of his mandate, shown clemency to all prisoners condemned to death, he let Bontems and Buffet, the Clairvaux murderers, be executed. Domestic affairs actually held little interest for him; he was much more involved in foreign policy.

With the help of state visits, private trips and exchanges of views, he built up personal rapports with his fellow heads of state and government. He got on well with Mr Heath and Mr Brezhnev, less so with Chancellor Brandt and President Nixon. European construction was not a panacea he held by, any more than world peace, but he knew how to play the game, disciplining himself to perform the leading role required of him in the generally disappointing summit of nine held in Paris.

In 1973 his diplomatic field of action was largely outside Europe. Regular meetings with his four main counterparts and other, less significant, leaders were the main means for it. In the same year he fulfilled a long-standing ambition of his predecessor, with a visit to China and meeting with Mao. In dealing with events in South-Asia and the Middle East during the global inflationary crisis of 1972 and the 1974 oil crisis he tried, not without occasional success, to be in the foreground, attracting the spotlight. At the same time he sought to maintain France's distinctive positions.

In the election campaign of February-March 1973 he shamelessly exaggerated the choices available. According to him these consisted of the misery of a totalitarian People's Republic on the one hand and, on the other, the freedom, progress and good life that come with democracy. As well as orchestrating the Majority's campaign he animated ministers and kept candidates on their toes. The Opposition was laid into with the natural force of a woodcutter going about his work. He won the election. The semi-defeat of the referendum was laid to rest, as were fears of the Left gaining power and doubts that had gathered around the Majority's durability. Notwithstanding the Opposition's admittedly strong gains, it still held forty more seats, which gave this alliance between the UDR and its Giscardian and centrist supporters a large enough margin with which to govern.

A long final illness

The president of the Republic's renewed vigour and determination, the dashing success he had just improvised: these were not to endure. He was already ill and worries about his health were draining him. During the winter of 1972-73 the Élysée let it be known that he had a recurrent flu. By the spring he did not look well. He was puffy, his figure somewhat gross. During his television appearance of 31 May 1973, fifteen to twenty million French viewers could see the transformation. Face-to-face with an alert, motile Richard Nixon at Reykjavik, his own swollen features and ballooned outline, the ponderous way he moved, his obvious lassitude, that made even speaking problematic, were stupefying. How he had changed! What was he suffering from?[14] What was going to happen?

From this moment, his extraordinary career would play itself out in an end-of-reign atmosphere. Without much subtlety the pretenders to his succession hovered around the tired leader, who oscillated between debilitated spells and managing to rally. Reassuring announcements on the state of his health plus evidence of being on good form alternated with engagements being cancelled and reductions in his workload. There was a contrast too between his intermittent, trenchant exercise of authority and the way that political life as a whole was now haphazard or static.

In June 1973, he committed himself, above all, and with the

determined drive particular to him, to the weighty but delicate issue of revising the constitution by a reduction of the presidential term from seven to five years. Why, one might ask, was he set on this reform? Did he envisage stepping down after five years – in 1974 – either to present himself for another mandate and a total of ten years in the Élysée, or was he considering his health and a final retirement? On the other hand, his intention may have been to fulfil his original mandate to 1976 and then serve a shorter second term? Nobody knows; perhaps he did not know himself, and wished to keep as many options as he could open.

The difficult manner in which, having chosen Parliament as the means to carry through the reform, he won the first vote in the National Assembly, suggested that when it came to a second vote in Congress, it would probably be defeated. Without further ado, he placed the measure, that had so recently been considered urgent and fundamental, into cold storage. This was a second failure, following the ineffective referendum in April 1972, and it seriously undermined the Gaullist dogma of presidential infallibility.

As the political class sensed the inevitable and started to plan for the succession, he increasingly appeared a sick, irritable man to his countrymen. They could see though that, in enduring his physical suffering, the head of state, who was still capable in bursts of acting energetically, showed great courage in the face of adversity. This was the final image the French people had of the man who met the challenge of governing them, following in the footsteps of the other man, who placed above all else 'La France'.

Georges Pompidou was born on 5 July 1911 in Montboudif (Cantal). He died on 2 April 1974 in Paris.

François Mitterrand

A Design of Life

The death of François Mitterand, president of the Republic for fourteen years, gave rise to lengthy obituaries. Here is a frank portrait of a complex man, who had constructed a novelistic life in the pursuit of his destiny. The writer suggests that if this adventure was a success, the presidential career was not. The greater part of the obituary is reproduced here.

(1996)

The distinguished-looking head, its stern features, which time and the man together in a long-term, if never fully completed, project had buffed to a high, almost harsh resonance: what linked it to the combative and voluptuous, haughty and unreflective attitude of an adolescent with dreams of literary pre-eminence? Who remembers the earlier, almost threatening and rebarbative face that seemed to suggest the gentleman thief 'Arsène Lupin', in whose guise Mitterrand 'mugged' the Socialist Party at the decisive Congress of Épinay-sur-Seine, as Pierre Mauroy put it? As if it was not enough for him to blur his traces as he moved, not just from one stage of his life to the next, but from being a certain kind of man with one physiognomy to becoming another, he also possessed, more than anyone else has in the political world, a virtuosity when playing in the following registers: a daring look that was cunning too, conveying his astuteness; beetle-browed with a downcast set of mouth; or, if the situation demanded, a luminous forehead and epicurean pout; feigning anger, a sharp outburst; (another look) secretly regarding prey; but, very occasionally, in moments when he briefly forgot himself, his natural facial expression conveyed a rather noble quality and revealed a man who was genuinely cultured. Finally, there was a sudden laser-ray-like sideways glance. It signified, in a conclusive manner, his total lack of indulgence towards other humans, bordering on meanness of spirit, as though he did not just have de Gaulle or the French Right to contend with, but found himself ranged against the whole world.

These self-created paradoxes tend towards perhaps the strangest, which is why an apostle of liberal democracy puts himself across as a Caesar. 'Dr Jekyll and Mr Hyde' is just the first of the clichés that suggest themselves and amongst which one can become a little lost; the number of different readings of François Mitterrand has become diverse and varied enough to match the preconceptions of just about everyone at some point. One simply has to help oneself.

Accusations of being a class traitor and of playing false by his tribe, of having no other rule of conduct than his own appetite for manoeuvring: the Right's essential view of him, with one or two variations, did not change. At the beginning it was Georges Pompidou who had reproached him for being an 'adventurer on his own behalf'. The argument later developed that he was actually a man of the Right, who had used the Left as the vessel with which to satisfy his considerable thirst for power. Having given him a leg up the Communists came to regret it when, long before the Berlin Wall came down, he destroyed them as an effective force in French politics. Subsequently, and with some reason, they denounced him as capitalism's willing flunky. The two socialist parliaments that bear his stamp will remain associated with a marked rationalisation, and quickening in the pace of, French capitalism.

Both sides probably took him too much for what he was not; or, at least not precisely: a man who was bound by neither beliefs nor principles. But it is likely that they also exaggerated his capabilities. In spite of taking wrong turnings more frequently than he would have wished, his reputation taken as a whole, continued its unabated growth, until he became the living idol of the socialist faith. As such he appeared to be a modern day Proteus or like Molière's 'Big Mamamouchi'.[1] He was the 'highest and most just'. Jack Lang, meanwhile, served as the high priest of a liturgy which compared the 10 May 1981 victory to an annunciation: ' "the freeing" of stifled energies; the return to individual authenticity; the mastery of a shared national destiny'. In a piece he wrote six months after the event, the minister of culture proclaimed that, 'on 10 May, the French People mastered its fears, to make a stand against received authority. It broke down the edifice of obscurantism, to let in reason in its place'. Michel Rocard's reading of the situation was somewhat different. In it, François Mitterrand was taken for an impostor at the top of the Socialist Party, whose mistakes, in both word and deed, had led the Left straight to defeat in March 1986 and to disaster seven years later.

'The world appeared good and in harmony to me'

So, what can one say with certainty about him? How does one

try and get to the core of such a complicated man? Seeing that the exercise of power is a crude encounter with reality, perhaps it is best not to try and delineate each and every nuance of his character. Above all else he was required to bear the burden of his office. Election by a majority in favour of his platform represented one responsibility. Then came the other, of trying to personify France; to represent the whole spectrum of French opinion, including the minority. He shifted, to an extreme degree, between the two spheres of his brain. One of these, representing the urge for change, was always capable of contradicting the other, pragmatic sphere. Change signified the volition to create and be present at some kind of era in French history; pragmatism took the form of wanting to be a philosophical protagonist who kept a constant watch on his action, correlating it to the conception which he held in his mind.

But even this gives an incomplete idea of his mental processes. He had in fact crafted several personas and these different aspects or versions of himself, whether they belonged to his public or private life, had become so rigidly ordered and set apart from one another that he could not always recognise himself any more. His original goal, to live his life as if it were a (philosophical) work in progress, had been waylaid in the process of a continual manifestation of himself – including to himself. Gradually, this permanent, increasingly suave, personification became self-perpetuating and usurped the earlier intention, to live his life as if it were a novel.

He had revealed his difference from the outset, when he wrote an article that criticised the Munich Agreement for *La Revue Montalembert* (edited by his fellow students at 104, rue de Vaugirard). This was at odds with the typical way of thinking amongst the young men at this Marist fathers establishment, whose family backgrounds were *bien-pensant*/Catholic/*petit bourgeois*. François Mitterrand had arrived at this Latin quarter address in autumn 1934 when he was eighteen years old, straight out of Saint-Paul's College in Angoulême. Here he had received his education and religious instruction not from theologians, as is commonly supposed, but from a combination of rural and diocesan *curés* and lay priests. At 'No.104', an address that was not liable to harbour dangerous revolutionaries, he subsequently got to know and move amongst right-wing students, who were mostly under the influence of Charles Maurras' nationalism. He also made some lifelong friends, the closest of whom was Georges Dayan.

Mitterrand was not from the working class. Born on 26 October 1916 at Jarnac in the Charente, he was the fifth child in a comfortably-off, bourgeois family of eight. His father was a representative for the Paris railway company, based at Orléans. On the mantelpiece of his presidential office Mitterrand kept a photocopy of his first railway employee's payslip. This employment ended three years after François was born, when he took early retirement, in order to deal with family affairs and, later, to become president of the federation of French vinegar manufacturers. Mitterrand's mother, Yvonne Lorrain, had grown up close to Cognac, the daughter of a notable. She was an austere and very pious Catholic woman. Between his home in Jarnac and his maternal grandparents' at Touvent, François was brought up in a religious atmosphere. He enjoyed a happy childhood. 'Papa Joseph', his own father, and 'Papa Jules' – or 'Grandfather Lorrain' – provided him with a stable, peaceful environment. He would recall later how 'the world appeared good and in harmony to me. My childhood was happy. I thought that it was natural for people to get on together, that friendship was for ever and that love lasted.' (...)

'My mother always used to say that war was caused by religion and nothing else.' Mitterrand was speaking to Vice-President George Bush, who had been dispatched to get an explanation from the French socialist president with the temerity to include communist members in his government. 'She was passionately for liberty and against revolution. As a child she instilled respect for the United States' Founding Fathers in me.'

Allowing for the fact that he was wooing the vice-president quite deliberately, these words reveal the profound and long-lasting basis of the French president's reasoned anti-communism and his visceral Atlanticism. (...)

His range of political influences was nothing less than eclectic. But it was writers that he was primarily interested in: Paul Valéry, Drieu la Rochelle and Giraudoux, Bernanos and André Gide. He devoured their works and would occasionally go to hear them speak. Still, the suspicion clings to him that during this period he belonged to the Far Right – according to some, Action Française, though others say Le Croix de Feu, or even La Cagoule.[2] 'What good does it do to try and prove one's innocence? None – by denying what they say, one simply reduces oneself to the level of one's accusers. Silence is better. Besides, I would rather have made my own political journey – if it were true that I was once a member of the Extreme Right – than be a part of the crowd that passed in the opposite direction.'

Against the Gaullists

There was undoubtedly misunderstanding about what ideology Marc Sangnier's *Le Sillon* championed.[3] In spite of its influence, the Church's role in society was in fact its specific concern, as it left other agendas alone. The very idea that Mitterrand had once been a *cagoulard* involved a misunderstanding because if, as Georges Pompidou said, he was an adventurer he was above all a rational adventurer and to be a *cagoulard* would not have been a sound choice. He may have been coming to political and intellectual awareness in a tense, heightened climate but it was his own personal destiny, rather than involvement in the immediate situation, that generally claimed the upper hand with him.

He was amongst the minority to accomplish what others dream about – through a stubborn concentration on this destiny, perhaps the only sure guideline in his life, he arrived at the point of living it as though he were the protagonist in a novel. Buoyed up by a deliberate, albeit instinctive, acquisitiveness of the mind, he succeeded in continuing with his personal adventure that was originally begun as a sincere, right-leaning Pétainist. This adherence to legitimacy, which the Marshal represented, would not turn out so badly for him, as he discovered his way in politics (at the same time as with women), concentrating on a determined conquest, then exercise and consolidation of power. There was never any doubt in his mind concerning his leadership role, which a commanding taste for both life and power suggested to him. The first time he played the part was at the now defunct 'No.104' where, each year, the students elected their own president. He was their clear choice on this occasion. This first victory was not long afterwards succeeded by his first defining experience as a young man, of captivity. Wounded near Verdun on 14 June 1940, François was then taken prisoner. Mitterrandian legend would have it that this was where he came to share with others the experience of poverty. Though it may well have been the case, the passage in *La Paille et le Grain* (*The Wheat and the Chaff*) where he recounts what was to become his famous survival on swedes, falls rather pat in its evocation of a young man, taken prisoner, discovering the virtues of socialism, notably the need for a certain ordering of society, in order to pre-empt its alternative, the law of the jungle. Being imprisoned was not a condition he bore lightly. Following two earlier attempts, he escaped from his Lorraine camp on 10 December 1941. Barefoot, he covered seven kilometres to a Bar Tabac in Boulay, where a cupboard provided him with a hiding place.

More than poverty, he was struck by the wartime phenomenon of treason. This followed his second defining experience, at a relatively young age, of ministerial office in the IV Republic. Between January 1947 and May 1957 he held eleven posts. (...) When fortunes in the Algerian War were running low and resignation was the order of the day, he decided to stay on. So, from the outset, he was against de Gaulle, and his political life was to be defined by their competing claims to legitimacy.

The rivalry was fundamental. Using his *nom de resistance*, Captain Morland, Mitterrand had to be almost forcefully restrained from attending the Hôtel de Ville on Paris' day of liberation, 25 August 1944. He was already going around calling de Gaulle a usurper. In fact he instinctively disliked whatever smacked of Gaullism. It is quite likely that this rivalry explains his allegiance to the Left.

The cause of his antagonism was that the Gaullists had hijacked the Resistance's politics and its values as well. Speaking to Alain Duhamel during the preparation of *Ma Part de Verité* (*As I see It*), Mitterrand argued that, 'the story has yet to be told of how the Free French guilefully stepped into the Maquis' shoes', adding that, 'it would reveal how their leader consequently appropriated credit that belonged instead to the underground resistance'. Accusing the General of a Stalinist rewriting of history he concluded sardonically, 'those services rendered to France that did not reflect glory on the General counted at best for nothing, and at worst were positively suspect'.

The accusation of being suspect was also levelled at Mitterand. In the eyes of Michel Caillau, another prison camp escapee and de Gaulle's nephew, this was self-evident. From their contested leadership of the prisoners dates the ill-feeling, it is commonly agreed, between François Mitterrand and de Gaulle. In Caillau's version of events, Mitterrand comes across as something of an arriviste, but even more as a Pétainist, evidence of which was that, when he was in London, he had received the Francisque, a Vichy decoration.[4] Mitterrand's recounting of this award was different: 'I was in London at the time I was given it in 1943. When I got back this acted as a useful cover.' It did not prevent a Vichyist label being applied to him. This culminated in his implication in the trial of the regime's former head of police, René Bousquet, for crimes against humanity. But, although he was director of information at the central bureau for POWs, Mitterrand moved in Vichy circles in which many officials and politicians were far from being collaborators, and a reasonable proportion considered it possible to undertake national reconstruction away from the occupier's gaze. These were men who partially succeeded in maintaining the state, if not actual sovereignty. Some of them would gravitate towards resistance activity following the period when everything was still unclear, 1940-42. This was François Mitterrand's case. Others continued to work for the regime.

The retrospective demonisation of Mitterrand as a Vichy thurifer, apart from its prejudice, is inapposite too. The truth of the situation is simple and straightforward enough: he and his colleagues, right-leaning for the most part and working within the regime, set up a consistently active resistance network. Their view of the regime was that the collaborator and true enemy was the head of the government, Laval, plus those who worked for him. The head of state, on the other hand, stood for a certain legitimacy. He inspired this future resistant to pity and chagrin before revolt. For François Mitterrand was much slower, during this sad period the country was passing through, to apportion blame than the Gaullists, with their systematic naming and shaming of traitors. He may have served Vichy in an official capacity, benefiting from the protection of a family friend, the journalist Gabriel Jeantet, who was a member of the Marshal's cabinet. And he may have received the Francisque. But, like others who fell in with the Maquis at the end of 1942, the nature of his resistance was not just bureaucratic; he was a genuine combatant.

A personal dispute with the General's niece, Geneviève Anthonioz, helped to consolidate the instant mutual antipathy that he and de Gaulle felt for one another. The General was particularly fond of this young woman who, following the Liberation, sat on his committee for deported women, which met in a requisitioned building on the rue Guynemer. This arrangement came to an end in 1946, when Mitterrand and another well-known resistant, Henri Frenay, intervened; their influence persuaded the Paris diocese to reclaim the property. The two government ministers then found themselves well placed to be amongst the first tenants there. Involving Geneviève Anthonioz, this cosy relationship was not to be forgiven. It went into Mitterrand's and de Gaulle's ledger.

The 'leaks' scandal

Competition for political position was tough amongst the young veterans of the Resistance, looking to press home their advantage. François Mitterrand favoured the RGR (Rassemblement des gauches républicaines) alliance of Socialist republicans, an inclusive grouping that welcomed a wide range of opinions and which tended to lean more to the right than its name suggested.

Standing as a candidate for this heterodox party on 2 June 1946, Mitterrand was defeated in elections to the second Constituent Assembly. On 10 November, he stood again in fresh elections and, this time, won a seat. He had drawn up a programme in the name of republican unity, which was against 'deficits, inflation and bankruptcy, administrative waste, costly and ill-thought-out nationalisations, and power-sharing with the Communists'. It was for 'private property, permitting private education, and eliminating unproductive employment'.

François Mitterrand's entry into politics was evidently opportunistic. What he had going for him was an appetite for and ability to acquire power. It was as Pierre Mendès-France's minister of the interior that a third decisive moment, the 'leaks' scandal, irrupted into his career.

The government was one that he had largely helped to fashion. When asked by the new prime minister whom he would recommend for the Interior Ministry his response was, 'Me'. It was unfortunate that, so soon after he had taken up the post, he should find himself caught in an awkward spot, being accused of treason. Already, in 1953, he had resigned from the Laniel government in protest against a general being dispatched to oversee the Algerian situation. The stand he took was on the priniciple of abstaining from the use of force in North Africa. This followed the discovery, as he claimed, of injustices being committed within the jurisdiction that he had been responsible for as overseas minister.

His more recent difficult predicament stemmed from links he had developed with the editorial directors of *L'Express*, then entering upon its great period. He was held responsible, in his capacity as a member of the Defence Council, for security leaks to the Soviet Union. Although it was discovered these came from a senior official, his own innocence did not prevent him from being the target of a smear campaign. With some justification he felt himself the victim of a conspiracy. The sense of isolation that this induced was heightened by an absence of support from Pierre Mendès-France, who had failed to give any warning of the suspicions that were gathering around him.

At the centre of the conspiracy was the former deputy, Pesquet, a long-term source of information for François Mitterrand – mostly bulletins on the Poujadist movement when he was minister of the interior. The Gaullists' goal was to derail the careers of those IV Republic leaders who remained credible and an obstacle to their own progress. In Mitterrand's case they were helped by the minister himself: having given Pesquet his word that he would say nothing, he did indeed remain silent. It is now known that, for services rendered – placing himself at the disposal of the Gaullists, who were well aware of how Mitterrand operated – Pesquet was promoted to run the VAP in the Lower Normandy region.

Proving just how resilient he was, Mitterrand came through this tricky ordeal. He would go on to survive the IV Republic, with a solid entourage convinced that he still had a destiny to fulfil at the national level. The foundations of his political reputation were now in place, thanks largely to his method for dealing with the Algerian question, that had been a masterclass in ambiguity: depending on the context, he propounded opposing policies. In private, within the circle of government, he was for incremental change; in public, he was for war. On the one hand, he convinced Mendès of the need for reform in Algeria; on the other, he could be blamed for the communist Yveton's death. 'The only means of negotiation is to wage war,' he said in 1954. Unlike a de Gaulle or a Mendès, with him nothing was matter-of-fact.

Nothing, that is, other than a political strategy that would make him not only the strongest opponent of de Gaulle, and the V Republic he was now constituting, but the Left's unchallenged leader as well. (…) It did not take long for Mitterrand who, thanks to the voters of Nièurre, had in the meantime sought alternative, Senate, employment, to work out the nature of the regime that resulted from the 1962 reform for presidential election, by direct, universal suffrage. This presidentialisation of politics required the Opposition, meaning the Left, to compose itself anew. Employing all his skills as a political strategist, Mitterrand subsequently devoted himself to the single task of gathering the various opposition forces for his leadership.

In delivering itself over to François Mitterrand the Left demonstrated its collective naivety. A man who elevated his own exercise of power to the level of a system had no difficulty in exploiting it. The inherent contradiction of their relation stood at the heart of Mitterrandism: a whole tribe – the Left – identifying itself with the plans and destiny of one man. From now on these were tinged with cynicism.

The gentleman thief and his helpers

To change or to conserve? The priority for François Mitterrand depended on circumstances, the balance of political forces and other indefinable factors. His opinion was that a political leader should stick to a handful of broad principles, so as to signpost his position to the public. (As Edgar Faure had previously put it: 'To know whether I am to the Left or to the Right, take a look at who is attacking me.') Beyond that it is a matter of negotiating events as they present themselves; if one comes to a crossroads then, by invoking one of the conveniently nebulous principles, it can be made to look as if a course is being held. Mitterrand liked to maintain the conviction that had him in the Great Tradition of the Left's leaders and, like them, of being in the front line ('look at who is attacking me...'). If this ongoing portrayal could occasionally appear a little heavy-handed that was because he was active at a time when ideology governed the world. It did not harm him though that he was a past master when it came to choosing the best ground on which to fight the battle of ideas. This was a further paradox, given his exclusive taste for novels. But, in spite of his lack of enthusiasm for original works of political philosophy, he revealed a natural talent in its practice. (…)

Once he had gained control of institutions giving him the freedom to act more or less as he liked, Mitterrand was unable to resist for long the temptation of monopolising position – the Mitterrandists differed little from the Gaullists and Giscardians who had come before them and, with a growth in presidential nepotism, via political appointments in administrative posts and clientelism pure and simple, one might even say they were worse.

Not coming from the Left, Mitterrand's relationship with it revealed his keen sense of friendship, as he bestowed largesse. The fact remained that he always harboured, vis-à-vis the movement, a feeling of illegitimacy. In 1971, the day after the Épinay Congress, in which Mitterrand and his supporters (including Pierre Mauroy) had defeated Alain Savary's wing to gain control of the new Socialist Party, Mauroy, who was to be his first prime minister, exclaimed, 'It's Arsène Lupin, the gentleman thief and his partners in crime'. From a left-wing perspective, Mitterrand's papers were never in order. One only had to look at his background: a Catholic, monarchist upbringing; cultural leanings towards the right; then the long IV Republic ministerial career, as minister of the interior when the Algerian War began and minister for justice, as it developed, unable to do anything about the series of summary executions meted out by the military authorities, and powerless when left-wing intellectuals, such as Georges Plavau, were put on trial.

He made no concessions when compensating for this lack of legitimacy, because a perception that had him belonging to the Right could not be allowed to form. This was why he felt so sensitive to attacks coming from the Left, but positively bolstered when delivered from the other side. (…) If contradictions appeared within either the official or private power structures he had erected around himself, he was the only one, standing at the centre of everything, who was permitted to resolve them. Although he did not try to resolve them – preferring that they became part of his identity as he lived with, and even profited by, them. The others were obliged to adapt 'as best they could'.

When, in June 1984, the battle over private education reform culminated in a demonstration of two million people convinced that the Left wanted to undermine all alternatives to state education, he knew that his government was heading towards a heavy defeat. But he certainly did not want to appear as the defender of 'priests' schools', already having to contend with the circumstance of his sister being nothing less than the secretary of the Catholic Teachers Association. So he waited for the protesters to perform their task of discrediting the ill-judged legislation, before imposing his decision that it should be withdrawn. In 1981, there had been an earlier example of his methodical insouciance, as he allowed a swathe of unrealistic promises, heralding the Left's arrival in power, to be made: the important thing was to consolidate his legitimacy with it.

A successful personality; unachieved socialism

François Mitterrand's victory in 1981 did secure his legitimacy with the Left. His re-election in 1988 showed that he was now accepted not just by his own camp, but by a much wider cross-section of the electorate. His various successes in presenting 'a certain idea of himself' ensured, as history will later confirm, that he could assert himself in either, albeit contradictory, stage of each presidential term. First came the socialist years, succeeded by the presidential resistance he put up during two years of cohabitation with the Right. Then, having been re-elected, with the opposition in disarray, he was finally able to savour the luxury of an uncontested hegemony. It did not last and, once again, he became the subject of criticism. The conclusion of his second mandate saw him dealing the best he could, as he was cast aside by changing opinion.

The range of his overall personal success had long served though as a prompt for a natural tendency to believe himself infallible, which was taken up and maintained in the type of court atmosphere traditionally reserved for a monarch. While on the surface he was courteous and kind, even friendly, gradually he became remote. So an already bleak view of humanity was reinforced by the passing years, with their accumulation of trying situations. He did not feel any compassion and tried to detect, on the basis of gestures and little details, evidence of his friends', just as much as his enemies', potential treachery, at the same time as he kept a constant lookout for their flaws and weaknesses.

But to focus exclusively on his powers of recovery (for example in the wake of 1984's noisy crisis or dealing with the 1986 cohabitation), his tactical astuteness and skill at manoeuvring, would be to draw an incomplete picture. If he had been without a strategic vision altogether, or had lacked an adequate understanding of the nature of both the V Republic and the Left, then he would probably not have arrived in the position to exercise these secondary skills, having first seen off numerous rivals before 1981 – Guy Mollet, Pierre Mendès-France, Gaston Deferre and Michel Rocard – who did not share his extra capacity. And, later, Jacques Chirac...

It would still be fair to conclude that, if the presidency was a personal success for François Mitterrand, for the Left any final audit of these years is liable to be disappointing: the undeniable achievement of a personal destiny in one column, but, in the other, the collective defeat of an ideology, for which he had been taken as the high priest. Whilst he showed himself capable of rising to the highest office from the moment he set his eyes on this prize and then, having attained it, of rising to the occasion, the ideas that carried him so high would be jettisoned in favour of the pure exercise of power.

From full-blown socialism to a measured capitalism

Governing at a time of structural change no doubt contributed to Mitterrand's singular destiny: he was left with little choice but to 'manage capitalism' as appropriately as possible. (...) The combined subjects of nationalisation and the state sector provide a good example of the ideological path that

Mitterrandism took. Campaigning, he had presented them as the key to change, symbolising 'rupture' and capable of being used as a lever for a radical redirecting of the economy. In 1981 the president therefore set about large-scale nationalisation, initially targeting banks and insurance companies. The principal aim was to gain a hold of the financial and industrial establishment that, until then, had helped guarantee the Right its control over French capitalism.

Nationalising Paribas and Suez the president perhaps abandoned himself to the moment of holding 'capital' in his grasp.[5] Three years later Pierre Mauroy was desperately trying to keep a cap on the figure of two million unemployed; nationalisation was duly presented as the means by which French industry might be preserved, with new management providing fresh motivation, and the means to be supplied by state expenditure. But in 1986, the first cohabitation was marked by Jacques Chirac's privatisation programme; so much so that, although triumphantly re-elected two years later, Mitterrand chose to pragmatically preserve the status quo, using the catchy 'ni-ni' slogan: 'neither nationalisation nor privatisation'.

The nationalising programme around which the Left had gathered in the first mandate was exchanged in the second for its opposite, privatisation – both a rebuke to the previous Socialist government and a symbol of Mitterrand being less the master of events, more their servant or accomplice. His 'ni-ni' encapsulated the transition from 1981's old-school socialism to the moderate capitalism of 1988; from arriving in power with a pledge to transform society, to maintaining his position being the overriding aim. Not that his second mandate was completely devoid of defining policies. François Mitterrand, after all, is likely to go down in history as the man who both made sure of

France's identification with the European project, sealed by the referendum vote that ratified the European Union's institution, and also as the leader who accompanied the movement towards German unification and the collapse of the Soviet Empire – two events that he would not have imagined taking place in his own lifetime. If one had to choose one date from each mandate, then 1983 and 1989 stand out. The first of these marked Mitterrand's Bundestag address, which was delivered at the height of the Euromissile crisis. From the crisis' hub, he proposed that the deployment of the Soviets' SS-20 missiles demanded a potential European riposte. One saw the best side of Mitterrand that day, as he unhesitatingly identified the possible aggressor, using the memorable phrase, 'the rockets are in the East and the pacifists in the West'. The French president's call to 'revive the flagging spirit of resistance' of Europeans was taken to heart. Once he made his stand on this point of pride, diplomacy towards Brezhnev's Soviet Union then stiffened and showed a greater purpose. With the view that West Europe could not live in freedom under the Soviet Union's cold stare, Mitterrand showed leadership at a key moment. Others would follow, in a test of strength that the West went on to win. At the beginning, however, public opinion had scarcely been aware of the gravity of the situation.

The high point of his presidency came in 1989. That year's bicentennial 14 July celebrations, a succesful blend of III Republic pageant and modernity, were his own triumph too. They mixed classic military march past with a carnival-like crowd, co-ordinated by Jean-Paul Goude, and a gathering of what were still – just – known as Third World leaders. Everything conspired to make the day stand out as a memorable occasion: his re-election the previous year was at the expense of the Right, which found itself at its lowest ebb, and the 'Second

Left', always a rival, had now been brought within his camp, thanks to the appointment of Michel Rocard as prime minister.[6] It was not so strange that the president might think himself infallible. Nevertheless, this was the year when history intervened, to waylay him and overturn his plans for something akin to a Directory of Three – held by France, Germany and Russia – towards which he considered the European situation might, with his assistance, evolve. His sense was of Russia, under Gorbachev's leadership, developing gradually towards a type of social democracy, and of Germany being prepared for a Social Democrat government, initially inexperienced but able to serve its purpose.

The wider historical moment that François Mitterrand contemplated, of a social democrat movement standing on the threshold of power, was not unreasonable either. In Madrid, Felipe Gonzalez's socialist leadership remained uncontested, while the dominant force in Italian politics was Bettino Craxi; in Germany, Oskar Lafontaine and the SPD appeared ready for office, whereas in Britain it seemed likely that Margaret Thatcher's rule would not continue much longer; Mikhail Gorbachev's, on the other hand, could. More than at any previous moment in his career, Mitterrand believed his and a triumphant Left's hour to build a social democrat Europe had arrived. One knows that this is not the way things turned out: people-power in the East rendered the political landscape unrecognisable, as it brushed aside the existing order and perspectives. From now on, all that was left was 'to take history as it came'.

François Mitterrand was born on 26 October 1916 in Jarnac (Charente). He died in Paris on 8 January 1996.

Jean-Paul Sartre

The History Man

'To be both Spinoza and Stendhal' was the great undertaking Jean-Paul Sartre proposed to himself. During the course of a lifetime, from *Nausea* to *L'Idiot de la Famille* (*The Family Idiot*), he would develop and clarify his radical perception of what it means to be alive. 'It was a privilege to live at the same time as such a man,' the writer recalls. 'When I first met Sartre he was sixty. His fame surpassed that known by any French writer, alive or dead.'

(2005)

When he was young, he was known to his friends as 'the little fella'. This was perhaps an ironic way of suggesting they knew a great destiny awaited him. His own view, from the moment he was able to guide this destiny himself, was no different. Raymond Aron could recall the admiration his small companion's assurance inspired – it was not out of the question that he would be the next Kant or Hegel. Aron said the question was often raised among his generation of Normaliens: which of Sartre, or his inseparable friend, Nizan would be the one to first become famous and who would achieve an enduring fame?[1] Sartre himself considered that he would be an important philosopher and that Nizan would leave a trace in literature.

Already, when he was young, he was projecting himself into adulthood and living his life, he revealed, as though he were the 'Young Sartre' future biographers would write about. His project, to be both Spinoza and Stendhal, reveals even more clearly the scale of his ambition. When she met him, in spring 1929, Simone de Beauvoir was attracted by this style of conviction and by his non-stop production of ideas and concepts; although his essays, when he asked her to read them, struck her as lacking in order.

The circumstances of Sartre's birth were what turned it, for him, into the starting point of a metaphysical adventure. What is a natural enough accident for everybody touched something essential in him – as far as he was concerned he might equally well not have been born. When, in *Les Mots* (*Words*), he came to interpret his rather particular childhood he wrote that, 'by hazard, my birth was linked to a death: the few drops of semen required to give life were in this case those of a dead man'. He candidly admitted that his father's early death freed him, as an orphan, 'from being imposed upon by either a cankerous power', or the supervisory demands of a superego. This gave rise to a strong-willed, even excessive character, and Sartre's intuition that his was man's natural state.

His own birth, in short, produced a philosopher of liberty. His personal experience as a small child then told him that man has no goal, other than that which he is at liberty to propose to himself. This type of (self-) assurance tends to give a man a head start in life.

The human condition viewed radically

So as to give his breakthrough the universal validity that its truth merited, he had to find the correct form in which to present it. Sartre now devoted himself to this task. He was conscious of his peers' progress: Aron, with a mastery of Kantian idealism, was able to pick his own theories apart one by one – but not to convince. Also an accomplished player, Aron spent his free hours on the tennis courts, while Sartre continued to plough his own furrow. For him the relation between his work and who he was was total.

At the same time that Nizan was able to draw on his experience of PCF (Parti communiste français) activism and solidarity with the damned of the earth to mount a, fictional, charge against the bourgeois enemy of humanity, Sartre had remained faithful to Valéry's neo-classical influence in his first full-length philosophical work, *La Légende de la Verité* (*The Idea of Truth*), even as he tried to give a new meaning to history as it was actually experienced.

It was on the advice of his companion, 'Castor', as he liked to call Simone de Beauvoir, that he set to writing about the influences that had formed him in a *Bildungsroman*, or coming-of-age novel. Dispensing with false modesty, he referred to it as a 'Testimony of Contingence'. For Castor the first draft, written in Le Havre at the same time that he was teaching philosophy, bore too strong a whiff of the classroom and she instinctively turned away. Why not, she then suggested to the author, add some of the suspense that at the cinema and in American novels they both took pleasure in? In Berlin, where he had gone to study Husserl and Heidegger in the original, he reworked the text completely. The academic year was 1933-34 and Adolf Hitler was consolidating power.

Beauvoir was still not convinced; he later described her as one of those merciless observers that nothing escapes. The manuscript was called back for further work, comprising cuts, rearranging and stylistic changes. Even with these improvements, Gallimard would not accept *Melancholia*. Sartre took the rejection personally and, when the attractive young lady he had fallen for refused his advances as well, he sank into a depression. Crabs and lobsters, he thought, were pursuing him and he diagnosed himself with chronic hallucinatory psychosis. All of which was vexing for Beauvoir, who reckoned her partner was positively indulging this madness. Giving up the psychotic posture, he got Charles Dullin, who was a mutual friend, to put in a word for him with Gaston Gallimard.[2] Proposing the title *Nausea*, Gallimard accepted the strange novel and the author consented, in good grace, to tone down its more provocative and vulgar aspects.

The rest is well-known: a critical success, the book narrowly missed winning the Goncourt Prize; novellas followed, as well as stimulating news pieces and articles for the *NRF* (*La Nouvelle Revue Française*), including one on Mauriac that the bemused Catholic writer was completely unable to respond to.

What was it Sartre offered that was new to the literary world in the 1930s and which would then make such an impression after the war? Going beyond politics, it was a radical perspective of who we are, that went to the ontological bases of the human condition.[3] Once a man reflects on his experience in a fundamental way then he will inevitably be ill-at-ease. He is never at liberty to be himself, and is instead caught between being an observer or the protagonist of whatever he does. The observer cannot be on easy terms with the actor and vice-versa. This means that an individual's consciousness is turned away, or liberated, from himself.

'Intentionality' is the name given by Husserl (the phenomenological philosopher) to describe this outwards orientation of consciousness towards objects. Man lives not just a part, but all of his life outside, exposed to the blast of events. Belief in an inner life must be banished, as the idea that it is possible for individuals to cultivate a unique personality is a vain myth. The liberty that phenomenology confers, even as it 'makes nothing' Proust's and psychology's twin worlds, comes via imagination, an aspect of consciousness that leads out towards the objective world.[4] This freedom does not come for free: the implied responsibility – one that it is impossible to evade without dissembling, in bad faith, to oneself and to others – is of the highest kind. But there can be grandeur in an engagement with the outside world and a freeing from all determinisms, including that of the unconscious.

These key themes of Sartrian, or atheistic, existentialism – seen in contrast to the Christian existentialism that originated with Kierkegaard – first appeared in various writings published during the 1930s. The war offered Sartre the opportunity to both develop and deepen them. Their full conceptualisation and formal statement came in 1943 with the publication of *L'Être et le Néant* (*Being and Nothingness*).

The century's liveliest and most agile intelligence

It might appear a merely contrary remark, but the war was Sartre's biggest break. Written in the first days of the Liberation, his essay *La République du Silence* begins with the famous first sentence: 'We were never more free than under the German occupation': because it was a limiting one, this situation defined the extreme choices to be made.

Sartre was to be criticised, especially after his death, for offering only a sedentary resistance, rather than taking up arms, as Jean Cavaillès and René Char had done. He was never shot or tortured. Sartre, in short, was guilty of being Sartre. Of having written *Les Mouches* (*The Flies*), *Huis Clos* (*No Exit*), *L'Être et le Néant*, rather than killing Germans or blowing up trains. He may have come to reproach himself for this choice but coming from others, especially those who have profited by reading him, the charge is ludicrous: Sartre the writer's resistance is hard to fault.

Criticism of the political stances he took in the aftermath of the war, in the 1950s and '60s, and the manner both in which he justified and hardened them, is more admissible. Even then, the objectives he set the Rassemblement démocratique révolutionnaire (Movement for Revolutionary Democracy) in 1948-49 can be favourably contrasted to his reasons for being a fellow-traveller of the Communist Party between 1952 and 1956. First he wanted to give substance to democracy's abstract ideals in a European polity, at once socialist and revolutionary; later he chose to defend the party unconditionally, as the repressed representative of working class interests. Seeing that it was less well armed in the Cold War, the Soviet Bloc, he argued, was more anxious for peace.

At the same time, the positions he adopted were never purely political: we should not forget that Sartre's work during these contested years was (in the eyes, for example, of Bernard-Henri Lévy) that of a genius. *Les Chemins de la Liberté* (*The Roads to Freedom*) was itself a test, via literary experimentation's means, of liberty, in the style of American novels' subjective realism. Then in *St Genet* he undertook a grand-scale existential psychoanalysis of his fellow writer. The question of what happens to humans living their historical moment is pursued with élan in a series of plays: *Les Mains Sales* (*Dirty Hands*),

JEAN-PAUL SARTRE

Le Diable et le Bon Dieu (*The Devil and the Good Lord*), *Les Séquestres d'Altona* (*The Condemned of Altona*). In these and other *works – La Critique de la Raison Dialectique (Critique of Dialectical Reason), Les Mots, L'Idiot de la Famille* – the complexities man is confronted with are rendered intelligible by the alert and supple regard of the twentieth-century's foremost intellectual.

To be alive at the same time as Jean-Paul Sartre – stirring and funny, a good companion – was a privilege. He was sixty when I first met him and his fame surpassed that which any French writer, living or 'immortal' had known; nevertheless his first concern was the other: me, you. He took pleasure in the stands you made, the hopes and projects you nourished. Still energetic, he was not really conscious of being 'Sartre', that doppelgänger whom, it vexed him, the Nobel Prize jury wanted to make marmoreal. He was happy to take life as it came, did not fool himself, nor tell the truth to those who did not want to hear it. Tears and regrets were not his style. Throughout our acquaintance he looked to the future and did not succumb to the pull of his past, even when his powers were, ultimately, on the wane. Whilst most men and women are answerable to particular interests, Sartre remained solely 'committed to the ideal of being uncommitted'. He remained free, and remains free now that, so effective in life, he is dead. His essential message is what is left of him, a spirit at large in history, moving amongst the intimate cluster of men, who were never more free than when open to his ideas.

Jean-Paul Sartre was born on 21 June 1905 in Paris, where he died on 15 April 1980.

Raymond Aron

A Distant Man

He and Sartre were friends at the age of twenty. Following the war, spent with de Gaulle in London, political differences would estrange the two Normaliens.[1] Sartre became the Left's intellectual idol, Aron the model theoretician and commentator of power, only ever appreciated with warmth towards the end of his life. This posthumous portrait, in honour of the hundredth anniversary of his birth, traces the development of a philosopher who was full of both insight and intellectual pride.

(2005)

Raymond Aron came out of Paris' Palais de Justice. He stepped into the car that was waiting for him, then, without a murmur, passed away. He was seventy-eight. That day (17 October 1983) had been spent giving a lengthy testimony in favour of the political thinker, Bertrand de Jouvenal who, before joining the Resistance, had, briefly, been a member of Jacques Doriot's Fascist Party. The historian Zeev Sternhell now accused him in a book of being 'pro-Nazi'. In the witness box, in his calm voice, Aron elucidated this substitution of a fast-and-loose version for the historical truth.

Many years before, Sartre liked to box while Aron played tennis competitively, the equivalent of a county player. The choice of these different sports, the sweet science required in an exchange of blows versus the fine calculation of angles from either side of the net, suggests much about their practitioners, now at rest in the same Montparnasse cemetery. They were two major thinkers in a century dominated by ideology, whose approach was almost entirely different. On the one hand Sartre, representing lyrical generosity; on the other, Aron, who rose above all partiality. In reality there was a great deal of emotion beneath the latter's (apparent) control. Those who knew Raymond Aron well describe a sensitive man always on the alert and frequently ill-at-ease. The tense, practically unremitting effort that self-control required of him bore little connection with the legend: that of an almost detached spirit, loftily serious. The Left, where he had made his beginnings, was to get to him with its ongoing baiting and criticism. Splits with Sartre, whom he never ceased to like and admire, and with Pierre Bordieu, his one-time research assistant were hard to accept. He never recovered from the personal tragedies of one daughter being born with Down's Syndrome and a second dying shortly afterwards, aged six. His other, eldest, daughter, the sociologist Dominique Schnapper confides that 'he struggled alone with his despair'. She, like her father, conveys a combination of gentle sobriety and conscious engagement.

'Faced by Hitler, philosophy's choice need not be delayed'

What needs to be said of the 1924 École normale supérieure's freshmen photo that groups together Raymond Aron, Jean-Paul Sartre and Paul Nizan, the philosopher Georges Canguilhem and the psychoanalyst Daniel Lagache? An unusually gifted year, whose ongoing debates Aron would nostalgically recall. The majority, including himself, belonged to the Socialist Party; all were ardent pacifists. Aron, born in Paris on 14 March 1905, would graduate top of the philosophy class, the same year that Sartre failed his exams.

Before discovering Max Weber, Léon Brunshvicg and Alain were his guides. At the same time that he was entirely occupied by philosophy, there was something nevertheless insufficient about the subject. During the course of interviews he made with Jean-Louis Missika and Dominique Wolton (*Le Spectateur Engagé – The Active Observer*, 1981) he related how, having left the École Normale, 'I really knew very little about the world situation or the latest scientific methods of enquiry. So I felt bound to ask myself what it was I was going to do; what was I supposed to philosophise about – naught? That was what lay behind my leaving France and all that was familiar here for something different.'

This happened to be Germany in the early 1930s. So, at the same time as deepening his philosophical studies, he witnessed the National Socialists' electoral breakthrough in September 1930. He did not require long to be convinced that, far from being a brief dalliance with extremism, the Nazi phenomenon could prove durable and dangerous enough to entail Europe's possible conflagration. Not everyone had the insight to foresee this outcome: though dominant by the time of his early-1930s' sojourn there, the regime left little impression on his friend, Sartre.

A further consequence of his stay in a Germany on the threshold of totalitarianism was the rousing of Aron's sense of racial identity. Born into a Jewish family which had fully assimilated within the French bourgeoisie, he now discovered for himself the origins that it had shed. Henceforth, he would make no secret of his Jewishness; a later attachment to Israel's cause would – somewhat to his surprise – be brought about in 1967 by the Six-Day War. His book *De Gaulle, Israël et les Juifs* (*De Gaulle, Israel and the Jews*, 1968) was informed both by the General's well-known characterisation of a 'self-confident people, élitist and overbearing' and, more importantly, the immediate menace threatening the Jewish state. 'By and by,' he would write, 'a sense of solidarity was formed, the exact reasons for which are perhaps not so significant. I can honestly say that if the Great Powers ... were to allow Israel, a small country to which I do not belong, to be destroyed, so too would be my will to live.'

One (apparently anodyne) encounter that took place soon after his return from Germany in 1933 also made a lasting impression on Aron. A friend, to whom he had divulged his anguished state of mind at the prospect of 'the nationalistic fury about to take hold of peoples *en masse*', subsequently arranged for him to meet with an under secretary at the French Foreign Ministry. The minister listened to him, then posed the question: 'But what exactly would you, who have just spoken to me so convincingly about the growing danger in Germany, do if you were in my place?' Aron was unable to respond at the time but would thereafter be persuaded that 'with a Hitler, philosophy is not obliged to weigh up each and every consideration'. And nor could political analysts be satisfied with the posing of questions.

With his political family, the Left, came the first signs leading to an eventual divorce. Aron had voted for the Popular Front in

1936.[2] He remained 'broadly speaking, socialist' and gave the government his assent, at the same time as he freely admitted its economic programme's lack of realism. As for himself, he appreciated 'having always been prone to mixed feelings, not least in relation to public events'. The legendary detachment of Aron, his daughter explains, dates from the troubled 1930s. It was in fact the outer expression of the struggle for mastery he pursued within himself.

This kind of inner conflict marked his ultimate falling out with Jean-Paul Sartre. Between covers since his 1938 *Introduction à la Philosophie de l'Histoire* (*Introduction to the Philosophy of History*), Aron had regained Paris and caught up with his friend following the war which, without ever becoming a Gaullist, he had spent by the General's side in London, making his debut as a journalist. He now provided leading articles for *Combat* and, in a brief collaboration with Sartre and Beauvoir, Merleau-Ponty and Malraux, co-founded *Les Temps Modernes* (*Modern Times*).

Next came a similarly brief experience of government, when he joined Malraux's staff. He was a supporter of the RPF, which opposed both communism and the IV Republic's constitution.[3] On 29 June 1947 began a thirty-year association with *Le Figaro* as an *engagé* commentator. At the end of his career he would move on to *L'Express*.

Splitting intellectual circles, the Cold War was to be the context for Sartre's and Aron's parting of the ways. Showing the same perceptiveness as when he had unhesitatingly grasped the nature of Nazism, Aron was quick to recognise the Soviet regime's basic character and to offer his support to the Atlantic Alliance. Sartre meanwhile wrote that 'to qualify as an anti-communist you have to be a cur': there could be no moral justification for the other's judgement on Stalin and the USSR.

Aron faced a future without allies. Already spurned by the Left, a large section of mainstream conservative opinion had difficulty in accepting him, shocked as it was by his speedy recognition of the need, and support for, Algerian independence. Placed in an awkward position vis-à-vis *Le Figaro*, it was *Le Monde* which instead published lengthy extracts of his essay *La Tragédie Algérienne* (*The Algerian Tragedy*, 1958), with its revolutionary import.

In between the writing of *L'Opium des Intellectuels* (*The Opium of the Intellectuals*, 1955), a scrutiny of the Left's belief system, and *La Tragédie Algérienne,* Raymond Aron succeeded in upsetting, one way or another, the greater part of political opinion. A reformist in a volatile epoch, he satisfied neither of its revolutionary or reactionary counterparts. His panoramic view noted the century's commitment to ideology, analysed totalitarianism, and tackled both Marxism and crimes committed in the name of revolution head on, whilst pondering the related subjects of war, strategy, and the balance of power. But in an intellectual climate that the universities fostered, where Sartre was idolised and Althusser arbitrated, his rational approach and criticism were not particularly welcome.

He would nevertheless hold posts at Sciences-Po, the Sorbonne and the Écoles des Hautes Études en Sciences Sociales (EHESS) and, finally, a professorship at the Collège de France. At the Sorbonne a band of acolytes attended his seminars in the rue de Tournon. As well as Jean-Claude Casanova, who co-founded the periodical *Commentaire* (*Commentary*) with Aron, this included Pierre Hassner, François Furet and Dominique Schnapper, Alain Besançon and Pierre Manent, plus a smattering of highly intelligent East European emigrés: François Fejtö, Pierre Kende and Alexandre Smolar. All were 'Aronists' but not doctrinally so, since that was not their teacher's way. They were concerned rather with certain principles of political justice: 'Truth and precision were more important than passion'.

May 1968's *bête noire*

Aron's opposition to the Left reached its climax in May '68. He was not impressed by the university's effective closure and the state's inability to act when faced with the students' revolt, that targeted him as one of its *bêtes noires* and which he execrated. His former student, André Glucksmann, one of the movement's key actors, interceded to reason with some of his fellow revolutionaries who, armed with petrol cans, intended to go to the rue Tournon, 'to set Aron's seminar ablaze'.

'Aron found May '68 hard to grasp,' conceded Jean-Claude Casanova, one of his most faithful disciples, regretfully. His way of understanding had its limits after all. 'Analysing political and economic, diplomatic and strategic issues he had no problem at all, but his preoccupation with drawing out logical conclusions meant that he was less well attuned when it came to a, difficult to define, social malaise that could only be explained in vaguer, cultural and generational terms.' Aron's strengths and weaknesses when faced with this new reality struck Daniel Cohn-Bendit in a somewhat different way. 'He did not understand the role, necessary to politics, played either by popular will or the desire for freedom. Concerning 1968 he was nevertheless right about certain things. The tendency of the movement's own organisation towards totalitarianism did not escape him and the development later of its institutional democracy can be traced to Aron's thought.'

Gradually, anti-totalitarianism made an impact on the Left. The 1974 publication of Alexander Solzhenitsyn's *The Gulag*

Archipelago helped give validity to Raymond Aron's grand analyses of the century's ideologies. 'I said what needed to be said; no doubt it should have been expressed with other emphases,' admitted the philosopher to his daughter. 'The young generation requires to say it too, in its own way.'

It had taken all this time to bring about a reconciliation with his old friend 'Poulou'. The occasion was presented as left-wing intellectuals declared their solidarity with the Vietnamese boat people, escaping from that region's gulag. A Sartre-Aron deputation was suggested. On 26 June 1979 the previously irreconcilable pair went to the Élysée, without having to be asked a second time, to argue for the cause. 'Aron,' remembers André Glucksmann, 'was perhaps the more affected of the two. He appeared particularly contemplative. Sartre, who was already blind, attached less significance to the meeting.'

They proposed the authorisation of three thousand visas to President Giscard d'Estaing. According to Glucksmann, 'having shed a tear', the head of state deigned to agree to one thousand. Aron and Sartre were free to leave, as they had arrived, side-by-side. The same spirit of urgency that, in the early days of *Temps Modernes*, had united them in the face of a suffering world had acted upon the two, older, men once more. Sartre showed his indignation; Aron offered his analysis of the crisis, which he summarised with the phrase: 'They forget how History is tragic.'

For Raymond Aron there remained just enough time to finish his *Mémoires*, published a month before his death in September 1983. A few more years and he would have lived to see the fall of the Berlin Wall. For Dominique Schnapper, 'that is a regret. With his faith in human liberty he deserved to see it'.

Raymond Aron was born on 14 March 1905 in Paris, where he died on 17 October 1983.

Robert Doisneau

A Poacher of (Extra-)Ordinary Moments

Doisneau's world was not that of international assignments but of Paris' boroughs. His reputation, which was assured by the 1980s, remained independent of the whole world of influence, luxury and wealthy women. A certain number of his photographs, notably *The Kiss by the Hôtel de Ville*, have attained a niche in the popular imagination.

(1994)

Robert Doisneau, who has now died, was more than just a photographer; he was a sociological phenomenon. The diffusion of his images transcended the area he worked in, to become household items. How many postcards sold? How many posters chosen for a home or an office wall? Everybody, it seems, knows *The Kiss by the Hôtel de Ville* which is the best-selling photo of all time, not to mention *Mademoiselle Anita at La Boule-Rouge* or, having sounded the alarm, his scarpering street kids.

'A "Doisneau" ' is the instinctive reaction to his images, just like 'a "Cartier-Bresson" ' or 'a "Lartigue" ' is to theirs. There are others who, coming after him, can be equally rapidly assessed as 'School of Doisneau'. For those who like labels, he is not hard to identify as a humanist. His popularity – Aragon considered him populist – can be explained by his manner of drawing out the charm possessed by fleeting moments. He did this in what he called 'my little theatre', a field of action that he limited himself to not because of technical considerations, but out of choice and because of the anthropological appeal it held for him: 'A chestnut seller in the Place d'Italie is worth more than a king's ransom.'

His milieu was sharply defined: Paris' neighbourhoods, her suburbs that rubbed shoulders with the city. This was the teeming slice of life where he liked to wander or hang around, not being in any particular hurry, rather like a student goofing off classes; a world where 'trouser pockets were unencumbered by spending money', whose natural light possessed an aura his photos would then obtain. Reportage of global trouble spots was not for him. Instead, as Prévert de Boubat remarked, he 'reported back on the world of peace'. Doisneau himself confirmed the aptness of this observation to his biographer, Jean-Francois Chevrier: 'History with a big "H" holds no interest for me.'

The newsworthy, enticing fields of operation which lay beyond the single one he had made his own – he left alone. Doisneau did not photograph landscapes or still-lifes or nudes. Well-respected men and influential women, the circle of power and conspicuous consumption were not for him.

Before opening the shutter, Doisneau always waited for the moment that he felt 'authorised'. He certainly would not force the door. On more than one occasion, he has described himself as a 'fisher, rather than a hunter of images'.

The nature of his catch? Given that the world his photographs conjures up is not a drily matter-of-fact one, it is not documentary evidence precisely. 'I am just trying to show, thanks to what, one imagines, is the incontrovertible evidence of a photo, that the world is – at least a little – as I imagine it and would like it to be.'

Doisneau has never made a self-portrait but, in a way, he does not need to: the photos are a type of self-representation, remarkably droll, human and apposite: a signature mark. He has frequently admitted that 'the only people I really feel able to photograph are those I have an affinity with'. Which is why he remained faithful to the suburbs; within a mile radius, first in Gentilly, then Montrouge, all he had to do in order to find a novel image was to alter his itinerary from day to day. Welcoming us one year ago to his studio/apartment he said that, over a sixty-year span, that distance has provided an average he was happy with. 'I've lived here since 1937 and am the oldest object in the house,' that 'is a clutter of books and objects,' its walls covered with paintings and photographs.

During this time the status, incarnated by Doisneau, of the photographer has radically changed. As part of the street scene, he was unclubbable; since, he has become revered. He has a characteristic way of describing this transformation: 'Formerly the photographer ate with the servants, now he dines upstairs'. In spite of which, the man who snapped *The Kiss by the Hôtel de Ville* remains part of that earlier generation of adept freelancers for whom photography was simply a craft. That was the way he was taught to regard it during his apprenticeship.

An industrial photographer at Renault

He was born on 14 April 1912 in Gentilly (Val-de-Marne) to a family of limited means. The area where he grew up, and subject of his first photo, was partial wasteland, weakly lit by gaslight. According to Jean-Francois Chevrier, it nevertheless left him with the lasting desire to record this childhood setting. Instead of fulfilling his father's hopes that he would become an engineer, from 1925-29 he attended L'École Estienne (École Superieures des Arts et Industries – Higher Institute of Applied Arts), qualifying as a lithographic printer.

Because of the scarcity of employment then, he took a job as a photographic assistant in Ullman, the advertising agency's, studio. He had a more active role from 1931, as assistant to the sculptor André Vigneau, who kept him busy taking research photos. He ran across Sougez and Tabard and married aged twenty, the same year in which he sold his first work – taken of a flea market – to *L'Excelsior*. Two years later he went to work for Renault, where he held a job for the remainder of the '30s. But he never became involved with the Popular Front. 'When they went on strike, I'd go canoeing,' he said.

Leaving Billancourt far behind, he took to the streets as a weekend photographer – a double existence he would continue for the next fifty years. 'During all this period,' he explained to *Le Figaro* in 1986, 'my better-known photos were invariably taken when I was moonlighting from my employers.' The photographic apparatus he initially used – a black drape, 9 x 12 cm wooden box and accoutrements – weighed twenty kilos. 'When I first got going in photography, wood still predominated.' But it was not long before such equipment gave way to the lighter and easier to operate Rolleiflex. As for his daytime job: he found it boring, was frequently late and, finally, in 1939, Renault fired him. As yet, little interest was being shown in his portrayal of the suburbs.

He joined the Rapho agency, which he would return to in 1946. At the same time he persisted in his extracurricular activities, which paid off in his first – and most successful – book *La Banlieue de Paris* (*The Suburbs of Paris*, 1949), with text by Blaise Cendrars. The appreciative writer penned him: 'It is important that this collection bears your mark. You are an original talent and you need to understand that.'

Fingers full of ink

The '50s were to be a busy time for Robert Doisneau. Advertising agencies and industrial clients commissioned him, as well as the press and mail order companies. He gave fashion photography a shot at *Vogue*, without fully having the aptitude for it. Much of this work was in colour and he carved a niche for himself as an illustrator. But even as he did so, he was more occupied than ever as a freewheeling photographer, working in the early morning, then after work, not to mention the weekends. His reputation was now in the ascendant. Braque, Picasso and Giacometti had their portraits taken by him, and Fernand Léger and Carné too. He was on easy terms with Cendrars and Marc Orlan and Prévert – whose café terrace photo, nursing a goblet of red, would acquire fame. Prévert dedicated some lines to Doisneau that the photographer acknowledged as a good description of his approach: 'C'est toujours à l'imparfait de l'objectif / que tu conjuges le verbe "photographier" ' ('The verb "to photograph" (an object) makes sense / in the language of the imperfect tense').

Following the publication of five books, the most recent being *Instantanés de Paris* (*Paris Moments*, 1955), that came with an Albert Pléay preface, a 'Doisneau style' had been established. Almost too emphatically. So began the (false) reputation, that still clings to him, as a purveyor of photographic fables. Whilst it is no doubt true that Doisneau likes to capture characteristic moments, which sometimes appear to have been prepared as elaborately as a practical joke – a schoolboy amusing himself by poking his finger into a classmate's mouth; a dedicated homeowner straightening out his lawn with the use of a rolling pin – his purpose is not to caricature: these moments' real meaning, as captured in black and white images, lies in what is left to the spectator's imagination, to his or her capacity to dream.

In common with other photographers bearing a 'humanist' or 'poetic-realist' label (Ronis, Boubat, Bovis, René-Jacques, Janine Niepce, Hervé, the Séeberger brothers, Frasnay...) Doisneau fell out of favour in the 1960s and '70s. Like them he was to be rediscovered in the '80s, since when recognition has been considerable: the award of Le Grand Prix National de la Photographie (National Prize for Photography) in 1983, and the publication of fifteen of his books during a ten-year period. Construction of a Doisneau museum is meanwhile underway in Gentilly. Sales of his postcards now total 2,300,000, the single image of *The Kiss by the Hôtel de Ville* accounting for 80,000. A poster of the same photograph has sales figures of 410,000. Two hundred limited edition signed prints of it have been sold at 22,500 francs apiece. His book *Fingers Full of Ink*, whose text is provided by Cavanna, has sales figures in excess of 250,000.

No doubt about it: Doisneau is in vogue. Such are the times that people are running after nostalgia, for a re-assurance that photography provides almost better than anything else. Statistics confirm his popularity. In a 1992 survey conducted by *Le Monde*, 31% of those canvassed said, 'they had heard of Doisneau', a much higher figure than when asked the same question regarding Lartigue, Cartier-Bresson, Nadar or Newton. He is unquestionably the most popular French photographer. It is not easy keeping track of all the films – including Sabine Azéma's *Bonjour Monsieur Doisneau* – and TV programs made about him. Doisneau is a gift for directors, with his natural raconteur's talent and range of choice self-descriptions: 'a poacher of everyday moments'; 'recorder of randomly thrown up elements'; 'sometimes the skewed perspective is the best'.

Authenticity rather than virtuosity

Within creative circles Doisneau's success was frowned upon. He was accused, on a number of counts, of a lack of rigour, of not caring when the press cropped his photos, nor showing any regard for original prints' value, by neglecting the number that were subsequently made. A similar attitude to profuse, often botched, exhibitions of his work was also held against him. With the exception of Oxford's Museum of Art in 1992, he was not the subject of a major retrospective in his lifetime. In line with these criticisms, his books were poorly produced it was felt: he did not seem to mind commercially motivated publishers blithely cropping his photos.

He remains, nevertheless, a photographer with a recognised body of work. Jean-Francois Chevrier's fresh evaluation has provided a better understanding of it, distinguishing between Doisneau the technician and Doisneau the artist. Dealing with the *canard* of him being a pedlar in nostalgia, his biographer places him in the tradition of another chronicler of vanishing Paris, Eugène Atget, with whom he shares the ability to evoke the city's photogenic genius, without falling for its picturesque lure. There is a similarity in their unaffected though decisive compositions which happily forsake virtuosity, and Doisneau has paid his respects to Atget on a number of occasions: 'There is a complicity that evolves between people going about their business in the same neighbourhood. What Atget captures is almost a throwback to rustic times.' Whilst admiring – from a distance – Cartier-Bresson's geometric compositions, he feels more affinity with Kertész and Brassai, whose *Paris de Nuit* (*Paris by Night*) really 'opened my eyes'.

This was the Doisneau whom François Hers, the project's photographic director, was persuaded to commission so as to record the suburbs for 'Datar' (Délégation interministérielle à l'aménagement du territoire et à l'attractivité régionale – Interdepartmental working group for regional and local development). The results were mixed: prosaically vacant vistas in subdued grey tones that would not have been out of place in a publicity brochure, but which were far removed from the lively work his name conjured up. In contrast to Henri Cartier-Bresson's quicksilver style, the other archetype of French photography, Datar proposed Doisneau, creator of 'studiously composed images'.

Little remains, that has not already been said, about this method. A section of opinion reproaches him with the regular use of 'actors' in his 'slices of life'. Doisneau tends to portray the relation as one of complicity between those he meets on the street and himself, to the point where he is indeed included, as orchestrator, in the photo. When questioned on this point he does not bother to dissimulate. 'There are a number of well-known images that I did set up. An example is the married couple in the bar. But this number is far less than is commonly imagined.'

The issue prompted *The Kiss by the Hôtel de Ville* court case. The plaintiffs, having recognised themselves as protagonists in the photographic scene, made a claim against Robert Doisneau for breach of privacy and commercial gain, which was how the public learnt that this mythical, natural moment between the two – he a would-be Yves Montand and she with something of Piaf about her – was in fact the coming together of two actors under Doisneau's direction: something the photographer had divulged to Jean-Francois Chevrier ten years previously. But no-one was listening, given the perception of him as 'the master of photographic impressionism'; the photo, being so closely associated with what one might call the 'wonder of chance' could not (until now) be accepted in any other guise. Although he won, the case marked him profoundly.

As the world moved on so Doisneau's previous grasp of it slackened. Images which before were his pleasure to catch – the streets, buildings and neighbourhoods as they had been, the old working life – had all changed. The familiar pattern of street cobbles had given way to tarmac. Paris as he knew it no longer existed. It was not only the physical world that had changed: attitudes were evolving and complicity being supplanted by reticence. In 1992 he remarked how, 'gradually, photographers became suspect', and that, 'I no longer feel accepted as I used to do. The spell has been broken. The space no longer exists for photographic bargain-hunters to conduct their freelance reportage'. This development, towards a world of professional photo-reporters, whose forthrightness he criticises, is not a happy one for him and is amongst the various reasons that, 'I do not enjoy life as I used to'.

Nevertheless, there are 350,000 negatives to show for sixty years of photography, more than a few of which are both extraordinary, and resistant to change.

Robert Doisneau was born on 14 April 1912 in Gentilly (Val-de-Marne) and died in Paris on 1 April 1994.

Henri Cartier-Bresson

Living Geometry

Henri Cartier-Bresson, a photographic innovator who inspired imitators everywhere, died at the age of ninety-five. He was one of the twentieth-century's geniuses. His obituarist recalled the lively spirit who liked to find the spot where he would least be expected.

(2004)

1995. Leaning on his cane in the weak light of the Musée des Beaux Arts in Bruges is a young man of eighty-seven, with a red scarf wrapped around his neck and a crystal blue eye pressed against a spyglass. For half an hour he remains twelve feet in front of Jan van Eyck's *Madonnna with Canon van der Paele*. It is good to listen to him enthuse about the faces' composition and the virtuoso handling of paint and colour. And it is funny to watch him disparaging the other visitors who hurry past with only a brief nod at what the painting has to offer. His death means that we have lost one of the greatest photographers of the twentieth-century.

Though, for the last thirty years this 'bag of nerves' has been working principally as a painter. 'It's a long time since I did any street photography.' A slight tease? Or, more probably, another paradox of 'wriggling eel' (his jungle name in the Scouts) linked to the mercurial intelligence which led him to where he was least expected? Amongst the puzzles he presented were those of being: an anarchist and a bourgeois; supporter of causes as well as a dandy; both a libertarian and puritan; naturally reserved though narcissistic; generous if hot-tempered; without academic qualifications but nevertheless unusually erudite... He autographs books 'HCB', but the fragile line of his fountain pen is well-known. He was famous for 'stealing' photos of people, a hidden approach out of which he structured an ethic, and resisted having his own photo taken. The more his work is exhibited in museums, the more he insists on his admiration for Van Eyck, Cézanne, Uccello and Piero della Francesca. Out of another marriage of opposites – his mastery of geometric form at the service of life as it happened – he managed to create a, much imitated, style of photography. It is hard to exaggerate his influence, even amongst amateur photographers for whom, consciously or not, the archetype of a successful photo is a Cartier-Bresson. Other professionals look up to him as a co-founder of 'Magnum', the original co-operative.

'I am happy to operate in an urchins' milieu'

A good photograph, Cartier-Bresson insisted, is the result of three elements. The first borrows heavily from surrealism: let chance take over, and engage with the 'maelstrom of life'; 'let the photo take you in its possession instead of you taking it'; record fleeting moments. The second requires one to judge 'the decisive moment' of this shifting reality. It will be the most intense and to capture it will involve body and soul – a teaching he found in a book which was amongst those that marked him the most, Eugen Herrigel's *Zen and the Art of Archery*. The final element is that the photograph's composition should be balanced in accordance with pictorial and geometric rules – the golden number – so that, even if inverted, it would not lose its aesthetic appeal.

The way to take the subject is by surprise – but without making him or her the object of ridicule, nor by stalking; the instrument is the unobtrusive and almost noiseless Leica. A photo should be black and white not colour, appropriate for fashion, advertising and the press but otherwise 'vulgar'. The combination of a 50mm lens and a 24 x 36 negative will record an instant most faithfully, while a soft and grey tint is the way to insure against overtly dramatic effects in a print. Its format should be small with a narrow black border to deter later re-framing. All these tenets were collected in Cartier-Bresson's key text, and perhaps photography's Rosetta Stone, *The Decisive Moment* (1952), which appeared with a Matisse cut-out cover.

Beyond these rules came practical experience; photography was a means of entry. In fact, it was almost a way of life itself, offering a passport to roam and to report back on the world. 'Form without a subject, without life is a dead end... I do not visit countries as a traveller, I am an inhabitant ... perhaps even an urchin. It is my way of operating, that suits me.'

A clairvoyant had predicted that he would lead an interesting life. He later shared the company of Aragon, Breton, Dali, Capote, Faulkner, Gandhi, John Kennedy and Marilyn Monroe. A string of his images became fixed in the imagination, often as postcards or posters: the Brussels peeping Toms, the first paid holidays by the sea, Marseille's homeless, King George VI's coronation, or the sad *Leap across a puddle, Gare St-Lazare*. At the end of the 1940s he photographed Gandhi's assassination and the Chinese Revolution. His portraits of the Joliot-Curie couple, his friend Giacometti, Matisse, Sartre, Bonnard and Mauriac achieved a landscape-like resonance as did the extraordinary, angular photo of the Brie region, resembling a cubist painting. There were one or two arresting nudes: Leonor Fini in the Mediterranean; lesbians in Mexico.

So far, there has been one authoritative appreciation. *Henri Cartier-Bresson: the Early Work* (1987) coincided with a touring exhibition that visited seven museums in the US. Its American author, Peter Galassi, marked off two periods in Cartier-Bresson's life and work, falling either side of World War II. In the 1920s the wealthy industrialist's son went to cabarets and brothels and ran across Breton and Crevel, Ernst and Dali. He was often in the company of the poet André Pieyre de Mandriargues, who described the period in *Le Désordre de la Mémoire* (*Unreliable Memoirs*): 'In nights that were often lively, we were searching for a release from the day's demands, an emotional charge … What I wanted, in effect, was that reality should let rip.'

This attitude was close to the surrealists', whom HCB spent time with once he reached seventeen. He was shy, very good-looking, elegantly dressed. 'Always sitting at the furthest end of the table', he listened more than he took part in the conversation. Like Brassai, he was cautious of manifestos, preferring to remain independent. As Rimbaud had, he travelled to Africa, where he hunted hippopotami. When he returned he felt ready to begin his work, 'with an instrument that would record the world's wounds at greater speed than a paintbrush. As a traveller I felt the obligation to record what I saw'.

From Italy to Mexico, the photographs that Cartier-Bresson took between 1931 and 1934 were to form the basis of his reputation. Often they were taken on the road, or in unwelcoming-looking spots, with a dazzling directness. They featured marginal figures, makeshift habitats. There is little doubt about them being modern masterpieces.

Occasionally the painter Leonor Fini came with him, while his most frequent companion remained Mandriargues, who recalls that 'driving around Europe, I saw the greatest modernist photographer come into being. It started off almost as a game, that became a natural activity for him. If others find themselves in the embrace of poetry when they are young he, the young painter, was taken over by photography'. HCB himself has written how, 'in a tense mood, I would spend whole days on the street looking for candid images that, once discovered, I took with the brazenness of a petty thief'. He had now become a surrealist photographer, which was how in 1933 he was exhibited in New York by Julien Levy.

Photojournalism is a sort of journal

More than once HCB spoke of how he was changed by the war and the burden of those times. Imprisoned, he succeeded in escaping. Robert Capa gave him a piece of advice: 'If you get stuck with a surrealist reputation, your work is going to become mannered. Become a photojournalist and you will be free to do what you want.' A new Cartier-Bresson was about to emerge, 'less of a dilettante, more of a professional'.

Over a bottle of champagne at New York's Museum of Modern Art he and Capa, Chip Seymour, George Rodger and William Vandivert founded the 'Magnum' agency. Their objective as a co-operative was to put photographers in charge: united they could withstand the influence exerted by magazines, and take the world as their oyster. For the next three years, Asia was the part that Cartier-Bresson handled, covering Indonesian independence, Mao taking power in Peking, and Gandhi's assassination, to name three stories. When detente eased open the door in 1954, he was the first photographer permitted entry into the USSR.

The illustrated press became HCB's principal source of income. He moved on from the 'decisive moment' to carefully considered reportage that was published, occasionally in colour, in *Paris Match* and *Life*. 'I became a colourist,' he reflected. 'I was very interested in reporting and loved to be on the scent of a story.' He emphasised how he had also remained true to his beliefs: 'My approach was still very immediate since, as far as I was concerned, photojournalism was a way of keeping a record of events.'

The geometric aspect of his, more lyrical, compositions grew, as if to bring a just order to the disenchanted world. Portraits, but only of public figures he respected, formed another part of his repertoire.

At the end of the 1960s Cartier-Bresson decided to reorient his career a second time. Instead of working with a Leica, he wanted to paint. For him it was a natural progression in the way he looked at the world. Round about the same time the photographer's reputation, fed by books and exhibitions, prizes and encomiums, was growing constantly.

In 1994 *Henri Cartier-Bresson:?*, a film by Sarah Moon, was premiered at the 'Rencontres d'Arles' ('The Arles Forum'). Its subject was there, keeping groupies at bay with another use of his walking stick. A 2003 retrospective at the National Library of France was a major success, attracting eighty-two thousand visitors in three months. This was also the year he became the first photographer to have his own foundation open, in an impressive modernist building situated in Paris' 14th *arrondissement.*

HENRI CARTIER-BRESSON

No longer active, except as an occasional teacher, Cartier-Bresson was now photography's star attraction. When he officially retired in 1974, Yves Bourde interviewed him for *Le Monde*. *Only Geometricians Need Apply*, as it was entitled, was a provocative statement of his aesthetic beliefs, to which a number of, vexed, photographers responded. The problem was partly his dominance in the field, that left others insufficient attention. Personally he had no wish to be referred to as the 'Father of French photography', while his insistence on painting's greater significance was unsettling. The National Museum of Modern Art (Centre Pompidou) had ignored him; it seemed there was something about France that rankled with him. It was in the United States that he had originally gained recognition, from 1933 onwards through the collaboration of Julien Levy, the gallery owner, and in 1947 at New York's Museum of Modern Art's 'posthumous' exhibition (Cartier-Bresson was thought to be dead).

Before he did actually die, he had a final word to say about his 'responsibilities': 'I am not responsible for anything! What does it mean anyway? Each one of us is free. How one leads one's own life: that is the moral question.'

Henri Cartier-Bresson was born on 22 August 1908 at Chanteloup-en-Brie (Seine-et-Marne), and died on 3 August 2004 at Céreste (Vaucluse).

Mgr Jean-Marie Lustiger

The Rebellious Cardinal

Jean-Marie Lustiger is a brilliant, demanding man of the cloth, who knows no rest. He is also a 'Jewish cardinal', an unprecedented figure as the writer notes in his examination, ten years after he was appointed archbishop of Paris, of a prelate whose authoritarianism and mysticism mark him out from the common run. Like an uncompromising sheriff he orders the bells of Notre-Dame to be rung, and dismisses hymns 'that have nothing to say'. Some consider him a possible successor to John Paul II.

(1991)

One is bound to ask: has there ever been a less ecclesiastical-seeming cardinal? From behind metal-frame glasses his eyes, radiating anxiety, suggest a constant state of alert, as if giving the lie to a bullish torso and chin. It is not hard to imagine him at night, in the almost silent mansion the archbishop occupies in the Faubourg Saint-Germain, expecting a crisis. An adviser tells how, 'when we are in a meeting and the telephone rings in the concierge's quarters, he, tensely, wants to know: "Who is that?"'

What is it that obsesses the archbishop of Paris, that accounts for a tragical delivery of his sermons? Is it fear of what the third millennium has in store for the Catholic Church? Or is it part of his cultural inheritance, the thought of Cossack horsemen bringing death to Central Europe's Jewish ghettoes?

It is ten years since his secret was revealed: born in France in 1926 to immigrant Polish parents, Mgr Aron Jean-Marie Lustiger is a Jewish cardinal.

The combination of those two words, encapsulating two thousand years of persecutions and disdain, is unprecedented. The public's reaction was one of curiosity; within the Church itself his uncompromising convert's faith was not so easy to accept. After all, a priest must take society into account, which might occasionally mean he needs to put his crucifix away in his pocket. Unlike his predecessors, Lustiger seemed to present an easy target for the party of Jean-Marie Le Pen and, more discreetly, some of those on the Christian Left.

It happened on Ascension Day 1940: making his way into Orléans cathedral, stopping in the transept, feeling touched by the grace of God. From that moment the relationship took precedence for the fourteen-year-old, who had arrived in Orléans from Montparnasse a few months earlier.

His father had been mobilised and his mother was obliged to keep their small milliner's business in Paris going. In the aftermath of September 1939 the parents wanted to find a safe haven for the two children, Aron and Arlette. At the crowded Loiret *préfecture* they encountered Mlle Combes, a young private school philosophy teacher. Asked by a *préfecture* employee whether she would take care of them, the discreet and kind Mlle Combes accepted.

'What should I do concerning Aron's religious education?' she asked.

'For now, nothing. We will see later.'

'And the little girl – should she come to my school?'

'Yes, she should.'

Aron was thus introduced into a Christian milieu. 'He felt as if he was amongst his own,' recalled Mlle Combes. For two years running, in 1936 and '37, his parents had sent him to Germany, where he stayed with a Protestant family for the summer, in order to learn the language. There had also been an occasion when, in a natural display of affinity, he had dug down in his family garden and sculpted Jesus' head with a crown of thorns.

Mlle Combes had no plans to convert him; she acted more as a facilitator for the divine mystery to find its course. 'I did not play any part; I was a witness.' It is unlikely he would have accepted blatant proselytising anyway. His contemporaries recall the young gentleman as a testy character, precociously reading and reflecting on Pascal's *Pensées*, which a teacher had lent him.

Mgr Courcoux baptised him and his ten-year-old sister in the bishop's private chapel on 25 August 1940. Aron was now, in the eyes of the Church, Aron Jean-Marie. His parents attended and, following tearful scenes that accompanied their earlier, firm opposition they were now convinced by the argument that, in the wake of the German occupation, being baptised might help to keep their children safe. The war contributed to the decision of this fundamentally emancipated Jewish couple, who had already deprived Aron of his bar-mitzvah, when they dismissed the rabbi who was preparing Aron for this event: he was considered too coarse and complacent.

On the move with false papers

He did not have to wear the yellow star, but only because his parents had had the foresight not to include him on the new census carried out by Vichy. All the same, his baptism did not guarantee his safety – at the lycée he was still Aron. One of the teachers cautioned him loudly: 'Do not think you are safe Lustiger. Because you are Jewish. Watch out!'

Unfortunately, this was all too true. In September 1942 Jean-Marie Lustiger's travels began. He moved first from Conflans to Decazaville before heading on to Toulouse. A period studying philosophy was succeeded by work in a chemistry laboratory with his father. He carried false papers and distributed copies of *Témoignage Chrétien* (*Christian Witness*). By staying on the move he and his father averted the worst; but his mother was informed on and arrested, taken to Drancy, then on to her fate at Auschwitz. After the Liberation he took up a place at the Sorbonne. He was a fiery student activist. At the 1946 UNEF (Union nationale des étudiants de France – French National Union of Students) Congress he was an advocate for the 'young intellectual worker'. He did not talk about his personal history – 'something between myself and my parents' – and no-one guessed amidst the general disorder of the time. Gradually though one or two perceived something different about him. The bishop of Dijon, Mgr Michel Coloni, who was his friend from 1945, recalled that 'he evoked his faith with an astonishing freshness – that of a convert'.

An avid reader of the furibund Léon Bloy, he, also, preferred to remain unmuzzled. The difference between himself and his future opponents was already being marked out. Whereas he wanted to shake and shift the Church out of its inherited contentment, they considered the Church's faith should generally remain hidden, rather like yeast acting on flour from within, until it naturally rose.

Tracing the gulag and Auschwitz back to Diderot and Voltaire

'His faith,' feels one of those closest to him, 'is Judaic'. Whilst Lustiger acknowledged his debt to his old teachers at Carmes seminary, where he moved on to from the Sorbonne, he reproached their successors for not always conveying God's grandeur. What he criticised was essentially 'historicism'. He demanded whether or not textual analysis of the scriptures, with its tendency towards relativism, risked unravelling, stitch-by-stitch, the entire Bible?

His own primary concern was a search for meaning. In summer 1951 he went on a pilgrimage to Jerusalem for the first time. Was it the Holy Land or Israel that he was setting foot on? Those he travelled with were unaware of the mixed joy and anguish that took hold of him as, with some pride, he visited the land his ancestors had originated from, and on which the new state had been founded in 1948. His baptism, he maintains, is something he had always experienced as a development of his Judaism, but it was now that he began to reflect more closely on this tie.

1954 was the year of his ordination – an unacceptable prospect for his father, who closed the door to him. Until the final moment it was uncertain whether he would come to the ceremony. When he eventually did he sat in a pew at the back of the church, rather than take the place reserved for him. For several years afterwards Jean-Marie would be careful not to wear his cassock when visiting the family home. His situation only came to be accepted later, by grudging and silent implication. It was on his deathbed that the father finally whispered the son's Christian name: Jean-Marie. Much to his satisfaction, Father Lustiger was about to be appointed chaplain to students at the – familiar to him – Sorbonne Centre Richelieu. For the next fifteen years his frocked figure could be seen riding a moped around the Latin quarter. He would often describe, most notably in his book *Le Choix de Dieu* (*To Choose God*), the Sorbonne of the 1950s as being marked by the 'post-war period's acute rationalism'. According to his friend, René Rémond, who was secretary-general of the JEC (Jeunesse étudiante chrétienne – Young Christian Students) at the time, this was not actually the case: there were a fair number of Christians at the university.

But if Jean-Marie Lustiger was rewriting history, it was in good faith: his occasional tendency to play fast-and-loose with dry historical facts, or to modify his own experience, is designed not just to exasperate specialists – as an amused friend relates, 'the moment he opens his mouth historians are on edge' – but to adapt them to his firm conviction, that Christianity finds itself in a hostile environment.

In this vigorous vein, just as he defends the Catholic Church from the Middle Ages onwards against charges of anti-Semitism, he holds the Enlightenment ultimately responsible for the twentieth-century's tragedies. To some extent, Diderot is the cause of the Gulag, and Voltaire, Auschwitz. If this argument creates an outcry by a majority of historians and philosophers, Lustiger is not concerned.

At a time when to be *engagé* was considered a virtue, he was quite deliberate in his posture of the 'withdrawn spectator' heading a team of chaplains. As for the situation in Algeria, his main preoccupation was to bring Muslims and Catholics together in prayer. 1968?[1] A non-event.

First and foremost: faith! He had no intention of altering his plans because Daniel Cohn-Bendit, alloying irony and invective, was in possession of Nanterre: the annual student pilgrimage to Chartres, scheduled for the beginning of May, was not going to be discarded because of the ephemeral events taking place; street protests would not upset a tradition that belonged to two Christian millennia.[2] As 'they' hurled stones at the so-called 'old' world, he organised prayer meetings.

Beefing up the liturgy

When Christian groups claimed to detect the pentecostal spirit moving amidst the chaos of the barricades, Lustiger changed colour. He admonished a group of students that they would be told to chant 'death to the Jews' – and that they would chant 'death to the Jews'. The sight of him refusing absolutely to allow them to open a stand in the Sorbonne quad was something to behold. And when the situation calmed he claimed: 'In a world that had lost all sense of proportion, we were the only remaining adults.'

At the beginning of June a meeting was held to ask the archbishop what position the Church should adopt. Lustiger was present and for two hours he remained silent, churning inside. Finally he had had enough: 'Your choice is between de Gaulle and the communists. Let me remind you that the last time the Church came out in favour of one side or the other was 1940. The archbishop of Lyon said: "Pétain stands for France". What is your choice today?' On that note he left, banging the door behind him.

Invited on another occasion to analyse what exactly was going on, he launched into a brilliant overview that prompted an increasingly bemused Mgr Marty to murmur into his neighbour's ear, 'a little cerebral, no?'

Without fully realising it, Jean-Marie Lustiger was out of step with the current episcopate thinking, typified by Mgr Marty's summation of this meeting, as he reached out to the younger generation: 'God is not a conservative.' It is possible that the student chaplain's unwitting disaccord led to a form of disgrace: in 1969 he found himself being assigned to the parish of Ste-Jeanne-de-Chantal in the heart of the 16th *arrondissement*. A different planet, where Latin mass was held in an incense-filled atmosphere. His successor at the Sorbonne, Mgr Jacques Perrier, reminisces that it would have been like 'living amongst the Zulus for him'.

Even as he abided by Vatican II did he lean too heavily on the Old Testament?[3] Several parishioners' complaints, not without a whiff of anti-Semitism, were sent to the archbishop. At the same time the suggestion arose – *sotto voce* – that he was a communist, an idea whose strangeness would not have failed to amuse Lustiger, who had spent May '68 doing whatever he could to counter *les événements*.

Feeling provoked, he set about changing things. 'You are mistaken if you come to Mass as if you were going to a petrol station, to fill up. You yourself are the fuel,' he told his alarmed parishioners. Decorative trappings were dispensed with; the liturgy was made more essential. In preference to hymns – 'frequently crass verses that say nothing, set to sentimental, vulgar music' – he favoured the psalms.

He did not think Christianity should fit in with 'society'. A particularly arrogant member of the congregation had his offertory cheque returned to him with the words, 'Your money does not entitle you to buy the Church'. There were other, more fruitful, encounters during his time in the 16th *arrondissement*: he met and became a firm friend of Jean Gelamur, the chairman of Bayard Press, whose home in the Basque country he would visit every summer. The meeting with the young philosopher Jean-Luc Marion, an exceptionally lively and capable Catholic, who would become one of his closest supporters and advisers, was also important.

The sermons he made during these years were preserved and soon collected for publication: as well as making the word of God known they would also cause Lustiger to be noticed. As a result he would not follow his ten years at Ste-Jeanne-le-Chantal, as he had envisaged, by joining an order in Israel and learning modern Hebrew; his destiny was to be otherwise. Without knowing it, he was being considered as a possible appointee by John Paul II, whom he had never met but who had received from Cardinal Bartoli, ex-nuncio in Paris, a highly favourable report. As if on cue, the bishopric of Orléans fell vacant in 1979 and the Pope designated him. This was how, thirty-nine years after his conversion, Aron Jean-Marie became one of the select few. 'For me – suddenly – the cross could bear the yellow star.'

Returning to Orléans, he was determined not to indulge in nostalgia. His bearing was stormy. Clergy and laymen were told not to mention the name of his predecessor during his ordination under any circumstances. Mgr Riobé had been a thoroughgoing progressive who dedicated himself to social and Third World issues. The new bishop's concern was faith, faith and faith again. Clearly, two different conceptions of the Church.

Rather like a country GP offering first aid out of a Gladstone Bag, he would make the rounds of his parishes with his chalice, paten and communion wine. Services were to be conducted according to no other aesthetic than his own: vases and flower arrangements should be removed from the altar. Vicars and *curés* were quick to learn to be deferential and to stand, respectfully, several metres apart when he was celebrating the Eucharist.

This may have been pride or simply a firm idea of his role. One vicar remembers him as an authoritarian figure. To another, who divulged some problems at a public meeting, he roared, 'Your problem is that you do not have faith!'

His time as a prefect-like bishop on the Loire was cut short on 2 February 1981 when John Paul II promptly appointed him to Paris. Archbishop! was something in itself, and also something to induce his anxiety. He looked to an inner circle of those he could depend on. In particular there was André Vingt-Trois, his *curé* at Ste-Jeanne-de-Chantal, who he now named his suffragan bishop and later his auxiliary bishop. Much of the Parisian clergy's Lustigerphobia would be absorbed by Vingt-Trois. Above all, his job involved keeping his chief in check. When a fresh problem presented itself, Lustiger's natural inclination was to act. 'What must we do?' he would exclaim. The trustworthy Vingt-Trois would sigh, 'Nothing – like normal. Wait a fortnight for it to blow over'.

The 'Battle of Wednesday'

His tendency to act alone grew, as he ostentatiously took to ignoring the advice of Vatican II's Presbyterian Council, whose purpose was to give democratically elected priests a voice in Church affairs.

Bishops were also treated cavalierly, for example during the 'Battle of Wednesday'.[4] At the same time that they were gradually working towards an agreement with the government for the Wednesday catechism to be maintained, he staked a trenchant claim during an interview for it to be held within schools themselves and so helped to torpedo the negotiations. Grinding of teeth ensued.

The next controversy was sparked when he initiated his own

seminary, the Mission of St Augustine, judging that seminarians were receiving too much instruction in the human sciences. This *démarche* was received in silence by the St-Sulpice seminaries of Issy-les-Moulineaux and Carmes. Their former pupil's disaffection was flabbergasting.

No longer could a *curé* be certain that his authority within a parish was sacrosanct. The archbishop, rewarding strong characters, 'spewed them' into positions around the diocese, so as to build anew. His words of encouragement to Alain de la Morandais, whom he had earmarked for the 16th *arrondissement* were: 'It is a rotten borough, brought to ruin by 'Action Catholique'. The Sulpicians, the Jesuits and other thinkers generally exasperated this more free-ranging 'intello', who had difficulty in disguising his preference for those charismatic movements whose devotion was not circumscribed by constant reflection. Any misgivings he might have had did not stop him from handing responsibility for Holy Trinity parish to the Emmanuel Community.

To mark the handover, the Catholic press was invited to spread the good news around. This clumsy advance was rejected. The two parties were already at loggerheads: being a convert, he held defrocked priests who took up Christian journalism in low esteem ('Why don't they become fishmongers instead?') and they, in turn, did not value him.

Speaking in a manner not commonly heard amongst the faithful, his strength in both Orléans and Paris was also his weakness. This prelate symbolised a confident Church that did not hold itself in check, in whose service he was frequently mystical, inspired and visionary. He spoke in earthy terms too, was not averse to addressing others, informally, *tu* or, losing his temper, telling them, 'shit!' and, 'enough of such stupidity!' The more that he was appreciated, perhaps lionised, by lay society, the more distasteful he became to the clergy. His frequent boredom in their company showed. Even when priest of Ste-Jeanne he would habitually be late for meetings held by the most gifted Parisian clergy, and would then make a point of sitting at the back, where he slowly made his way through *Le Monde*. When his book *Le Choix de Dieu* was published in 1987, both *Témoignage Chrétien* and the Jesuit *Études* (*Examiner*) examined it as though with pincers, at arm's length, in stark contrast to the secular press which was unanimous and unreserved in its approval.

Bernanos rather than St Paul

His taste for entering into debate with a variety of philosophers, historians and sociologists in the public eye irritated some of his entourage. As one wryly remarked, 'He will never refuse access to a *Le Débat* interviewer'; another, more bluntly, that, 'even when they happen to be talking rubbish, he is impressed by Emmanuel le Roy Ladurie's and François Furet's discourses on Catholicism'.

Just as he was more at ease debating with laymen than with his fellow priests, Mgr Lustiger had more to say about modern art or the Eastern Bloc Church – having experienced the division of Europe as an intimate issue – than his own diocese. In place of the article he had been asked for by Jesuits on the function of an archbishop in a great city, he submitted his thoughts on the subject *Man unbound, or: contemporary culture's great challenge*. The 'sacking' shortly afterwards of Father Valadier from *Études* was embarrassing for him; he was considered to have orchestrated this sanction when, in fact, he was neither for nor against it.

His appetite for debating with civil society was unaffected.

After leading the 1984 movement to preserve private schools came the build-up to the French Revolution's bicentenary: Jean-Noël Jeanneney, president of the celebration's organising committee was given a frosty reception. Point blank, the archbishop demanded: 'Tell me when republicans are going to finally leave off harassing Catholicism?'

That was his opening shot. The subsequent induction into the Pantheon of the Constitutional Bishop, Abbé Grégoire – 'unnatural' – naturally affronted him.[5] He was troubled by the prospect of these commemorations and planned to be out of the country in July. In the end he did attend the Paris celebration on the 13th. But the following day found him sulking behind the scenes. As for Jean-Noël Jeanneney, he is still at a loss as to why. 'It is the National Day!'

Denigrator of the Enlightenment, which he opposes at every opportunity, might he be an instrument of the Church's far right? Is it possible, as some claim, that he would consign Council's work to the waste-bin?[6] Such conjecture is perhaps not very helpful. The truth about Jean-Marie Lustiger is that he is torn between a sense of tragedy and arguments suggesting it may yet be overcome. It is as though within himself, without respite, the haunting image of the cross and the hope of the resurrection wrestle against one another.

Generally he finds that Bernanos' species of pessimism trumps the message of St Paul. This would have been the spirit in which he wrote his draft for the 1987 Synod of Rome's final message. Deemed too apocalyptic by them, his colleagues rejected both the vision and the draft. The modern world he sees all around him – a dumbing down through 'subculture"s medium TV; threats to the sanctity of life via abortion and genetic modification; violence – is one that is bound to concern this cardinal. It is an uncertain age, that does not prompt him to be a reactionary, as Réne Rémond rightly remarks, but to work towards a new era. This no doubt accounts for his resonance with the portion of opinion calling for the big topics to be debated in a manner that few are now prepared to admit – that is, by bringing norms into play.

It is not so surprising that he is one of John Paul II's favourites. At the same time, the familiar criticisms persist: of expressing himself too much and, favouring successive journeys abroad, of not concerning himself adequately with domestic affairs. He is often to be found in Rome, where he is particularly preoccupied with the appointment of bishops.

Does he envisage promotion himself? Vaticanologists are of the opinion that 'he resembles John Paul II too closely to be his successor' … perhaps. One might recall though the famous prophecy of the twelfth-century Irish priest Malachie, that the next papacy would have strong ties with Judaism. The logical conclusion of that long-ago forecast would be a pope who had converted from Judaism himself …

Mgr Jean-Marie Lustiger was born on 17 September 1926 in Paris. On reaching retirement age in September 2001 Cardinal Lustiger announced his intention to stand down. He was finally succeeded as Archbishop of Paris in February 2005 by Mgr André Vingt-Trois. He died on 5 August 2007.

Ayatollah Khomeini

The Supreme Leader

The man was a revolutionary throwback to the Middle Ages, and the inspiration of his people's overthrow of the monarchy. Convinced of being God's emissary on earth, his character was vengeful. He was hostile towards artistic expression – but not to bloodletting. When he died in 1989 he had ruled Iran for ten years, first as 'Guide of the Revolution', then in the terrible conflict with Iraq.

(1989)

It is rare for either a political or spiritual leader to make such an immediate, globally widespread, impact. There cannot be many left today unable to put the name to a face that might have been painted by El Greco: a spade-like white beard and mystic's penetrating regard, beneath bushy black eyebrows and a turban the same colour. The Imam Khomeini, supreme leader of the Shiite Muslims, was a revolutionary who came from the Middle Ages, a secretive man of few words – beyond his monotone haranguing of the crowd, in stark and effective idiom. While his exceptional force of character and his extreme obstinacy, that both unnerved and intrigued those around him, may have belonged to a religious leader, they also served the purposes of a highly developed 'political animal'.

Entering the final stage of his life he succeeded in mobilising an unarmed people, which then overturned the twentieth-century Pahlavi dynasty, in spite of its attempt to call upon two thousand five hundred years of monarchical tradition. In doing so, he also succeeded in humiliating the all-powerful America, which both supported the Shah and used its influence with him to maintain its position in the Gulf, the most important of all strategic regions.

The patriarch of Qom – one of Iran's two holy cities – had always been inspired by the will of God in his public actions. His, not always orthodox, interpretation of Koranic precepts informed the frontal assaults which, when he saw fit, he made on contemporary political and diplomatic structures. His messianic personality first intrigued and then disturbed the West; in Iran – particularly – and amongst the Muslims of the Arab world and beyond it brought him an attentive audience, ripe for the avenging message he preached in response to the humiliation of their recent colonial status.

His successive denunciations caused the majority of their leaders to tremble; according to him they lacked virtue, in the Latin sense of the term of 'manliness'; were preoccupied with their own interests to the detriment of the people's basic needs; and were insufficiently determined, when it came to countering imperialism from either East or West, as well as Zionism, 'which the Great Powers exploited and which served as the Palestinians' executioner'.

To Islamic society, torn between a return to its historical roots and accommodation with the modern world, he came across as an amalgam of Savanarola and Saint-Just.[1][2] Like the austere and forbidding Florentine before him, who had wished to bring about a change in morals by censoring dress codes, banning games and profane celebrations, and rooting out usury and luxury, Khomeini was anti-art: he condemned music because it softened the people, forgetting perhaps that the patriotic and religious songs they sang had influenced the insurrection against the Shah. He saw, as Saint-Just once had, a purifying virtue in bloodletting. The difference remained that, in his thinking about society, bloodletting was not intended to clear the way to the future but to herald a return to norms which had last held sway in the Arab world of the seventh-century.

A revered teacher

Ruhollah – a forename meaning 'Spirit of God' – was born in 1900 into a religious family in Khomein province. His grandfather, father and elder brother were ayatollahs. This family environment was to have a threefold political, religious and social effect on him, particularly when his father, Mustapha Moussavi was murdered by a landowner's henchman, following his involvement in the anti-imperial movement.

Ruhollah was subsequently raised by his paternal aunt, who continued to hunt down the assassin until he was brought to justice and executed. This was the strong woman who would teach her nephew that power was an equation of (more – or less – equal) forces and that Islamic principles could not be implemented on earth by persuasive means alone: they also required an unremitting pursuit of the opposing, infidel, forces. As he grew up, other significant events would mark him. First came the popular movement's success, obliging Mozzafar ad-Din to abolish absolute power in the 1906 constitution. The militant activism of the period's most respected ulama, the 'brave and incorruptible' Modarres followed. It was aimed against foreign, principally British, control as well as the doctrinaire modernising of Reza Khan's regime and the Pahlavi dynasty which, having overthrown the Quadjars, he then founded.

When he was fifteen, Ruhollah's aunt died. He continued his studies for a further twelve years, then began teaching at Qom. It did not take long for him to become one of the theology faculty's most prominent members or for his classes to draw its biggest attendances. The esteem in which he was held was not, according to his disciples, the consequence simply of his learning, but also of his 'moral stature'. As an adherent of *jihad*, whose principal meaning is not 'Holy War' but the struggle for self-mastery and improvement, the daily routine he proposed to himself was a strict one. Diet and prayer were the cornerstones of an ascetic way of life; a bowl of soup with a little bread was often all that would pass his lips, whilst five or six hours' sleep sufficed for him, as he continued with his nightly reading and meditation on the Koran. These were the elements of an intense spiritual activity. He made no distinction between religion and politics, as he worked within the Shiite tradition, that was based on the two pillars of the Imamate and of justice, and which had been concerned with the issue of earthly power from the outset. The celebrated Iranologist Henry Corbin compared the 'Koran, or the Imam silent, and the Imam, the Koran speaking', to signify that, in his role as a community leader, a Shiite cleric is obliged to ensure that justice is done. He must support the downtrodden against the oppressor, whether monarch, foreign power or simple individual. To do so, he will have to interpret the sacred texts so that they are relevant to the circumstances of the present time.

Imam Khomeini undoubtedly brought justice to bear, but with the country liberated from the Shah's oppressive rule and

American interference, the constitution of 2 December 1979 did little, apart from certain clauses, relating for the most part to the economy, to assure the rights of citizens and of ethnic and religious minorities. It instead took numerous liberties with them, reflecting the conservative attitude of the Shiite clergy, which five centuries of Islamic society's decline accounted for. Less conservatively, he realised, as other Third World leaders had, that national independence was the banner under which the fight against imperialism could be conducted.

'The Prophet was political!'

Throughout his life, his political engagement was invariably prompted by one of three converging themes: liberty, the rejection of foreign tutelage, and independence. He warned that the country was in danger: the Shah, who was the ' "Great Powers" instrument', represented 'absolute evil'. Ayatollah Khomeini's criticism of Reza Shah continued up to the moment the Allies, in 1941, influenced his abdication. The resistance he then offered his son, Mohammad Reza was harsher still. It took place across all fields – political, economic, social and cultural – until the Emperor's patience snapped. Khomeini was arrested on 3 June 1963. Large demonstrations were immediately held in protest and then unfolded in tragedy, as the principal one was broken up on General Oveisi's order for his soldiers to fire into the crowd. In the ensuing bloodshed there were ten thousand victims of the 'Butcher of Tehran', according to opposition claims.

On being freed in 1964, Khomeini resumed his verbal assault on the palace: 'How can you hope to modernise Iran at the same time that you imprison and kill intellectuals? The true way forward is not to turn Iranians into the willing and obedient victims of your authority and that of your own masters, the foreign powers, but to develop men with the ability to question and decide for themselves, courageous men who know how to resist pillage, injustice and foreign domination.' The famous 'Discourse of Qom' would later be quoted back at him when, at the hour of the Islamic Revolution's triumph, Khomeini's revolutionary committees – the *komitehs* – victimised the Left's lay opposition. At the time, this philippic earned him a Turkish exile. It was not long before Ankara, noting the demonstrations organised against itself, grew concerned and arranged for his consignment to the holy city of Najaf in Iraq, where his family was already based.[3] This was where he was to remain before it became Baghdad's turn to fear the consequences of Khomeini's continued appeals for the monarchy's overthrow, not just for its relations with Tehran but, internally, on account of the 50% Shiite population opposed to its own repressive regime of Ba'athist authoritarianism. The region's Muslim heads of state were now reluctant to play host to such a demanding personality, and his requests to them were turned down with the result that, the French government having discreetly obtained the Shah's agreement, on 5 October 1978 he found himself living in Neauphle-le-Château (Yvelines). Little did the Shah know that his opponent would show such consummate appreciation of how to handle the mass media.

Until then the written word was Khomeini's principal means of communication. Amongst his works were *The Greater Struggle*; *Islamic Government: Governance of the Jurist*; *Essays on the Islamic Republic*; *Fighting the Carnal Crusade, or: Man's Major Crusade*. Together they expounded his political philosophy, which denounced despotism as well as ruling classes that were themselves colonialism's subjects. He wrote that 'every time a man of destiny has arisen he has been killed or imprisoned, exiled or, at the least, anathematised, for presuming to enter the political arena. But what was the Prophet, if not political? Do not be taken in by those that disseminate falsehoods, who would exclude you from the political realm or the discussion of social issues. They are the same propagandists who would deny us the right of opposing our populism to the traitorous, anti-Islamic states. They wish things their way: to find no man standing in their path'.

Neauphle, the decisive encounter

An unexceptional suburban house with an apple tree was where the seventy-eight-year-old man's political strategy was to reach its intense and public culmination. The confrontation with Mohammad Reza Pahlavi was one he waged with unsuspected energy, to emerge the winner. Whilst the political class, including his future prime minister, Mr Mehdi Bazargan, was united in urging him to find some common ground with the American superpower, and to seek a compromise with the Shah – for example allowing him to continue as a figurehead or to abdicate in favour of his son – Khomeini was adamant: 'The monarchy must end.'

In December his long-distance orchestration of the Shiites' annual Ashura, an emotional commemoration of the martyred Imam Hussayn, assured that this political/religious event took on immense proportions in 1978. The palace suddenly appeared demoralised, as Khomeini masterminded a general strike which brought the country to a standstill and the government to the point of submission. An embassy of leading politicians travelled to Paris, hoping to moderate the Ayatollah. With the exception of Mr Chapour Bakhatiar, who had succeeded General Azhari when the latter resigned as prime minister on 31 December, it instead returned to Tehran having promised Khomeini its allegiance. Appointed by the Shah, the regency council's president would soon do the same.

On Tuesday 16 January 1979 the Shah and the Empress left Iran. But, if the Pahlavis were now gone, Khomeini had not yet abolished the monarchy as an institution. With the army's support, the prime minister continued to oppose the Imam's return. Then, as the crisis grew uncontained, he too came to terms with this likelihood. It was on 1 February 1979 that Khomeini made a triumphal entry into Tehran, where four million people, one of the greatest gatherings our race has known, came to greet him.

Having received his plebiscite by *vox populi*, he called on the Shah's prime minister to resign and, on 5 February, nominated a government headed by Mr Bazargan. The following weekend, during the Saturday to Sunday night of 9-10 February, the *Djavidan*, or 'Immortals', of the Imperial Guard, were so intent on 'handing a lesson' to the *Homafars* (Air Force officers) supporting Khomeini, that they failed to recognise they were in the process of triggering a popular insurrection set to last seventy-two hours: the 'epic three days'. They were to culminate, in the evening of 12 February, with the army's and monarchy's joint collapse. The latter's abolition followed seven weeks later, when the referendum of 30-31 March instituted an Islamic Republic. The subsequent election had barely begun before the local political climate deteriorated. If unanimity had marked the truly revolutionary phase, disenchantment and division had now worked their way in; the collective will was dispersed amongst fractious decision-makers.

Komiteh kept up an ongoing defiance of Bazargan's government which, throughout its existence, the Ayatollah himself was either criticising or disavowing, until 6 November

1979, when he accepted the prime minister's and cabinet's offer of resignation, on the grounds that they had paid too much heed to formal niceties and not enough to the revolution. Having repeatedly called in exile for human rights to be respected, Khomeini now gave a free hand to revolutionary tribunals, whose summary justice gave little scope for an accused to mount a defence. The existence under the previous regime of numerous victims of a similar style of justice in no way excused the new, religious, power's manner of dispensing capital punishment.

In France the Imam had vowed that the Islamic government would guarantee freedom of conscience and of speech. But, when the committees, claiming to act in his name, shut down 'non-conformist' newspapers and disrupted left-wing parties, isolated lay intellectuals, and struck women who were demonstrating to preserve their rights, he did not intervene. Instead of the egalitarian Islamic principles that he had formerly emphasised, ethnic minorities' calls for autonomy, in particular Arabs' and Kurds', were now met with repression.

Virulent anti-Americanism

This was the context in which Islamic students entered the American embassy and took fifty-two diplomats hostage, so as to precipitate the extradition of the Shah, then receiving medical treatment in Washington. Was the Imam behind this *démarche* or, realising the use he could make of it, had he covertly accepted it? No one knows. But whichever is the case, the action, that was without precedent in diplomatic history, represented a final means by which the people could be brought together in a common hatred of America.

The hostage crisis changed the course of the revolution: the regime's radicalisation accompanied the advent of an Iranian Shiite brand of Islamic fundamentalism – 'Khomeinism'. Clashes and incidents of murder became commonplace as *Komiteh Pasdarans* (Revolutionary Guard Committees), the basic unit of the 'Guardians of the Revolution', spread around the country. The Imam Khomeini instituted *Wilayat al Faquih* (Governance by Jurists), at the same time as he metamorphosed into the 'Supreme Leader' of the Islamic revolution. A position that, since spiritual power was concentrated in his hands and he was able to lay a firm hold on temporal power too, surpassed that of the Shah.

Abolhassan Banisadr, the candidate he supported for the presidency, was triumphantly elected on 15 January 1980. Eighteen months later though it was the Ayatollah, in alliance with the president of the Parliament whom he had dissuaded from standing, the Imam Beheshti, who finally caused Banisadr to be removed. Throughout this period Beheshti's Islamic Republic Party had manipulated the more radical situation, specifically the students, so as to discomfort the elected president. Banisadr clandestinely, and somewhat ironically, returned to France, where he had recently been one of the exiled Khomeini's most trusted advisers.

It is hard not to acknowledge the skill with which Khomeini's regime then proceeded to eliminate, one by one, any rival movements or parties. The first to go were the most vulnerable: lay student societies; white-collar unions; the league of human rights; the national front. The revolution, like others before, had embarked on its reign of terror.

For a while, with its support for the 'Imam line', the *Tudeh* (Communist) Party remained acceptable but, ultimately, it was unable to evade repression. The most activist movements were those spawned by guerilla fighting, the chief one being

Massoud Rajavi's, the *Mujahedin-e-Khalq*. On 28 June 1981 it wrought carnage at the IRP (Islamic Republic Party) headquarters. Amongst the more than one hundred killed by the explosion was the Ayatollah Beheshti, generally regarded as the regime's No.2. Two months later, on 30 August, came the assassination of both the Republic's new president, Mohammad-Ali Rajai and his prime minister, Mohammad Bahonar.

A type of *coup d'état*, these events seemed to leave the Ayatollah indifferent: it was not this way that Khomeini's conviction of being God's representative on earth would be eroded. Why should he believe himself anything less when, against the common expectation, he had consistently emerged victorious in the war he waged for Good against Evil? The evidence, after all, was there: the Shah had departed and his dynasty too; forty thousand American advisers had been obliged to pack their bags; the attempt by their Joint Task Force to stage the hostages' 'Operation Tabas' rescue had turned into the most pitiful of fiascos; and almost as pitiful was the failed plotting of Chapour Bakhtar and General Oveisi from within the army's ranks.

The 'Supreme Leader' therefore called new elections which, on 2 September 1981, brought Ayatollah Khameini to power. For the first time in her history, Iran's main offices of state were occupied by religious leaders: the president of the Republic, the prime minister and parliamentary president, Hashemi Rafsanjani were all members of the clergy, as were several ministers and the directors of key organisations.

From November 1979 the tone in which foreign affairs were conducted had continued to harden. Khomeini's and the mullahs' denunciations were given repeated airtime, so that all could hear about those Muslim regimes which were 'corrupt and traitors to Islam', specifically the Gulf States.

'The road to Jerusalem runs through Baghdad!'

Since he considered himself to be not only sanctioned by God but, in contrast, the target of an international conspiracy, Khomeini was persuaded to export the Islamic revolution. The deteriorating position at home contributed to his decision. Sensing a provocation, Baghdad decided to attack first.

Saddam Hussein's purpose in ordering the Iraqi army's 22 September 1980 invasion of Khuzestan (Arabistan) was to bring the Khomeinist regime to an end. In fact, he saved it. The Battle of Khorramshahr was to be the Imam's Valmy, prompting a profound and powerful Persian nationalism.[4] Khomeini's political adversaries swelled the ranks of those who came to the country's defence, as the war distracted attention that would otherwise have centred on the failure of its religious leaders to realise the Great Project, promised by the revolution, of a New Islamic Society. Economic shortcomings, meanwhile, were ascribed to the war.

Khuzestan's re-conquest began a year after its invasion, in September 1981, and was brought to a victorious conclusion in June 1982. Saddam Hussein subsequently proposed the laying down of arms, so that they could be taken up instead against the 'common Zionist enemy'. Disdainful, the Ayatollah's response was to give the order: 'The road to Jerusalem runs through Baghdad! Forward to Baghdad!' In continuous waves, his soldiers were launched over the top at the Iraqi defences. But 'miracles of faith' were no longer working: although war-weary and outnumbered three to one, the enemy resisted; Khomeini's appeals for Iraqi Shiites to overthrow the Ba'ath regime were not taken up.

Six years later, in July 1988, Iran finally agreed to a ceasefire. For the Imam it was a bitter blow. He compared it to having to drink poison. The costs of the eight-year Gulf War could be now assessed, in terms of one million dead and an estimated $450 billion expenditure. The war offered both an insight into, and was the symbol of rifts within the Islamic world, between the pan-Arabist Ba'ath regime – laicising, modernist, socialist – and pan-Islamic Khomeinism.

Ultimately Khomeini was not a builder of a new society but a leveller and a man of vengeance: revenge for the religious, whose power had been taken away by the Pahlavi dynasty (even if its modernising could be viewed primarily as a cultural abuse by Persian conservatives); revenge for Islam's Shiite minority against the always scornful Sunnis; and revenge against the Arabs who, converting Persia to Islam, had long ago imposed their language.

The power that, thanks to him, the Shiite clergy now enjoys is geared more to restoring what had previously been overturned than to creating a future for Muslims, which would permit them to live in harmony with the world. Imam Khomeini, the guiding light for one of the twentieth-century's most powerful revolutions, may transpire to have contributed to Iran's, and perhaps Islam's, regression in the twenty-first.

Imam Khomeini was born on 17 May 1900 in Khomein. He died in Tehran on 3 June 1989.

Karl Lagerfeld

The Elusive Dandy

Age, private life and details of his uncommon wealth are amongst the well-guarded secrets of the dandy-*provocateur*, Karl Lagerfeld. Fashion designer, photographer and publisher, Chanel's creative director is not quite the dilettante he would appear to be. His skilful, self-mocking defence is an asset of the legend, behind which the extravagant Mr K prefers to operate.

(2001)

Sushi, champagne, soul music: fashion's gilded world, in attendance for the launch of Lagerfeld's new perfume, is in effervescent cocktail-chatter mode. Then a sudden wave-like movement passes through the assembly, as though it was in a collective faint. A cluster of camera flash explosions marks the arrival of the domain's ruler. There is, of course, no mistaking him: the suit and shirt are black; the tie set in place with a pearl pin; powdered hair drawn back into a ponytail; spacious smoky-lensed glasses; his Spanish fan in constant motion. He circulates for the briefest of moments, with his aura that simultaneously evokes obscure European nobility and Molière's 'Big Mamamouchi': uniquely incongruous, moodily magnificent.[1]

The mere mention of his name is liable to produce either mockery or rancour, but the dandy it suggests is to be found more in photographic reproductions than in a tête-à-tête encounter, when he will, at least partially, put his persona to one side. A disdainful attitude towards what he calls the 'odious-visual' world, in which he has nevertheless succeeded in carving out a career, hides the mockery that, with the lucidity of the disabused, he directs at himself. Karl knows he is an introvert who must make something interesting of who he is; a big ego, if not self-satisfied; an 'amoral opportunist', who is nevertheless goaded by an 'essential, pronounced puritanism'. His laughter, that is never far away, coming in subdued bursts, serves to fortify him against 'self-destructing'.

There is an element of Gothic storytelling in the way he describes his family upbringing, hard to corroborate, in Germany, his country of birth. This event occurred, the official CV says, in a rural area seventy-five kilometres north of Hamburg in September 1938 – a date that, according to various facts and details, shaves a few years off the true one. His parents were relatively elderly. He has spoken of their 'strong moral fibre' and opera fanaticism, their being 'dyed in the wool' intellectuals who 'belonged to a culture which came to an end in 1933'. His father, Swedish by origin, was the proprietor of an import-export business centred on Vladivostok until 1917, after which Venezuela became the new hub of his commercial activity. Three fortunes were lost before his financial success was assured, importing 'Gloria' condensed milk products to Germany. Karl's similarly wealthy mother was a violinist, an imaginative personality who had 'little idea when it came to bringing up children'. Something of an afterthought to two older half-sisters, the young Karl was treated like a little lord.

His attendance at primary and, again, at secondary school was occasional, partly thanks to his persuasive way with words. Disliking the company of other children, this solitary, and self-professed idler, preferred that of adults or books: Homer, Jules Verne, above all the satirical magazine *Simplicissimus* and Aubrey Beardsley's illustrations. He was gifted with an 'elephantine' visual memory, that soaked up an impressionistic, not to mention impressive, marinade. When it came to creation: 'I had no formal training but I was born with a crayon in my [strange to say, powerful] hand.'

'The countryside was not exactly my trip but, at least, being a long way from the air raids and all the horror, we came through the war unscathed. With my six bicycles, I suffered no privations.' That did not mean that, by the time of the Allied landings, the family 'had not had its fill of Nazism'. 'We were happy to have English officers billeted at our property. One day there was a garden party to which Field Marshal Montgomery turned up in a superb duffle coat.'

For the fifteen- (+?) year old Karl, Hamburg was merely a port through which he could proceed to Paris. On arrival he settled down to a daily regime of three hours of French evening classes. His design for a coat won him the International Wool Secretariat's prize in 1954, while a certain Yves Saint Laurent was winner in the dress category. The two prodigious talents setting out on long careers were to share one another's friendship over the years, before their falling-out. Proustian Yves would spawn a myth and his own fashion marque at the same time that Karl, an inspired mercenary, offered his services to the great, established fashion houses. Someone who has known him for a long while hints that Lagerfeld might have been something of a Salieri to Saint Laurent's Mozart.

At Chanel

In 1955 Karl Lagerfeld was taken on as an apprentice at Balmain. Here he dashed off hand-sewn collections and absorbed everything the house archives had to offer. Within three years he was named creative director at Patou, where he developed both his technical skills and a feel for different materials, being instructed in double-knit and *tolle-ancienne* by Mme Alphonsine, whose association with Jean Patou dated back to the 1920s. These were the bases from which, with a facility acknowledged by all, his creativity would be directed. 'He is capable,' according to Gilles Dufour, his right hand man for fifteen years, 'of conceiving a collection's theme in the space of ten minutes.' François Lesage, from his vantage point as the Place de Paris' foremost embroidery designer, highlights 'the encyclopedic extent of Karl's culture: an entire century of design that he carries about in his head. That is the source of his originality. He has never been obliged to go along with the current fashion, be it Grunge or Destroy'.

The distance between him and his son did not lead Mr Lagerfeld Sr to sever the purse strings. 'I had accounts with the top shops for my suits and shoes. At twenty-one I was driving around in a Bentley coupé. The fact that I thought it completely natural just goes to show what a brat I was.' Every night, whether in Paris or St Trop', he would be at one of the cool nightclubs, a habit that lasted longer than ten years. A way, he said, 'of inoculating oneself against all future disappointment'. Another enthusiasm was weightlifting. 'With his wavy hair and dark allure one might have taken him for a gigolo,' recalls a friend of the time.

The Chanel years triggered off in 1983 when Karl Lagerfeld was appointed creative director of the haute couture, prêt-àporter and accessories lines. His insistent reproduction of the interlocking 'C' motif was not universally welcomed. Creating six collections a year he was able to introduce some of his own style – pink tweed, braiding, pearls – into that of the house Coco had originally built. At 29-31, rue Cambon, where little had changed since the days when 'Mademoiselle' used to sit on the mirror-lined spiral staircase, so as to check what was happening at every level, Lagerfeld, who could be both lazy and disciplined, diffuse and focused, produced his best work when under pressure, just as he previously had at the Fendi sisters in Rome or at Chloé. 'I am a terrible perfectionist,' he admits; 'fortunately the collections provide a deadline.'

Both the former managing director of Lagerfeld Ltd, Ralph Tolédano, and Yves Saint Laurent's mentor, Pierre Bergé prefer to offer 'no comment' on Karl Lagerfeld. Whilst Jean-Paul Gaultier may be 'taken by his performance', others prefer to walk on by. Fashion may be known for its endemic jealousy but, even more, it is a guarded world. The closest one comes to a revelation – in strictest confidence – is that the 'sun king' has too many footmen and is a little too fond of his own authority. Whilst claiming to only respond to others' jibes, Karl does like to let loose the odd cattish remark: 'Yves Saint Laurent has not done anything in twenty years'; 'poor Claudia [Schiffer], beautiful as ever, now advertising sexy little nighties that cost next to nothing'.

Whereas Saint Laurent has looked to Pierre Bergé, Lagerfeld is a latter-day Pygmalion. He does not have muses so much as 'his' creatures. First came Inès de la Fressange – 'as far as French elegance is concerned, she had it better than anyone'. Finding her 'amusing' he gave her the role of Chanel's lucky charm. 'I was the pampered one, for whom every imaginable string was pulled,' recalls Inès as she flicks, unhurriedly, through images of their collaboration in chic. 'I can see us now, out in the States for work and having to attend a gala night, with all the American women decked out in jewellery, which we nevertheless managed to escape from. I was in an evening dress and he was wearing a tuxedo. We climbed into Uncle Picsou's limousine and headed off to find a hot dog stand.'[2] Karl had said some pretty terrible things about her when she left Chanel in 1989; in return she gently ridiculed his 'Kaiser complex'. Today Inès comments on 'his non-interest in spiritual questions, and total lack of psychological empathy'; he has readily admitted to not having ' "opinions" or crises of conscience'; she preserves the memory of his sensitive and vulnerable side: 'without his dark glasses, one could see the boy he had once been.'

Following the Inès years, the Lagerfeld identity was expressed by Claudia Schiffer, who struck him as de la Fressange's 'absolute opposite, with her blondeness and healthy vitality, that reminded me of BB'.[3] In his eyes, she was an archetype. Speaking from Los Angeles, Claudia recalls their relationship in a very positive manner: 'For seven years we were working together closely. Karl is an extremely cultivated, generous, open man. He also has a wonderful sense of humour...' The man behind the 'Supermodel' phenomenon plays down his contribution: 'My métier is to choose a face; one that is suitably expressive'.

Because he has always, in his aesthetic fashion, loved women does not imply that he is either a sensual or a fickle man. The wound he endured in 1989, when the great affair of his life tragically ended, did not heal. Since then he has not, as far as his friends know, had any sentimental attachments. Embracing asceticism, he gets up at daybreak in order to read and maintain his, handwritten in ink, correspondence. He travels only because he has to. He has never smoked and does not drink, 'as it sends me straight to sleep'. Being sufficiently 'barbaric', his tipple is diet coke. In contrast, the simple pleasures of the table do not really interest him. From time to time he entertains at his eighteenth-century mansion in the rue de l'Université, but he goes out as little as possible. Society evenings, at which he remains alert to the latest news, have become a 'burden'. 'Following the Méry scandal I am an outcast.'[4] However, he has yet to lose the taste, that Balzac once had, for keeping company with a few exclusive names: Liliane de Rothschild, Laure de Beauvau-Craon or Caroline of Monaco, who is his neighbour in the principality.

Lagerfeld does not talk about his fortune. He states that the sale of his eighteenth-century furniture and art collection was for 250 million francs but that he has not decided how to deploy this money (if he is not to use it to mop up tax arrears). With the sale a page has been turned. 'In order to love something, it is not necessary to own it.' The old furnishings have been superseded by a minimalist style and 'screens everywhere'. As to whether he is involved in any 'good works' he remains discreet – and wary of foundations, 'like the one run by that ghastly pumped-up man raising money for a cancer cure'. Starting in 1987, the ex-prince of the jet-set has embarked on a further, photographic, career. With a battery of sophisticated equipment at his disposal, his work includes portraits of Jack Lang, Bernard Pivot, Caro de Monac' and la Cicciolina, the production of lovingly produced albums for a select few, and assignments published in leading magazines. His numerous critics point out that, 'trading on his name, he buys his way into these pages', and accuse him of plagiarising true photographers' work. His greatest remaining passion, that comes close to a mania, is for books. In the old days, 'La Hune"s shelves would be sparsely populated by the time he departed the shop. He has more recently opened his own art bookshop at No.7, rue de Lille, and founded a publishing house. As for his own 'legendary' private collection of a reputed 230,000 volumes: much of it is in boxes, following the sale of his Breton manor. 'I will donate them to a school or a university one day.'

Given that he is uninterested in holding onto old designs, how does this *faux*-dilettante assess his talent? 'It is by not latching onto passing fads,' he says, 'that I have been able to continue through all the different changes in taste. No doubt I have not pushed myself as I could have done,' he admits, at the same time as taking a snipe at stylists who 'portray themselves as suffering artists'. In his sixties and still in good shape, the extravagant Mr K continues to cultivate his nonchalantly frivolous persona, showing no apparent interest in nostalgia. What does remain for Citizen Karl is his own Rosebud: furniture from the old childhood bedroom, that he has religiously conserved and amongst which, on certain nights, he goes to lay down his ego and spleen.[5]

Karl Lagerfeld was born in Hamburg, Germany on 10 September 1938 (?).

John Fitzgerald Kennedy

A Man of Goodwill

John Fitzgerald Kennedy was assassinated in Dallas on 22 November 1963. His obituarist was still in a state of shock as he remembered the occasions when he met the young American president, including at the White House. 'His charm was his simplicity of manner.' Introduced without fuss or ceremony in the Oval Office, 'this foreigner had difficulty in recognising that he was sitting opposite the leader of the most powerful empire the world has seen'.

(1963)

Kennedy was forty-six, but he could have been ten years younger. This youthful appearance and attitude is what were most striking about him on a first encounter. His rangy student's physique did not have an ounce of excess fat and, rare for a politician, he had a fresh laugh. His face was not exactly handsome but, beneath the intrusively thick fringe and above a rather heavy jaw, his piercing eyes ensured that it left the true impression of a young leader. It seemed that he was made for happiness, like the lady who contributed so much to his success but, who is now crying over her murdered husband, her baby who is gone.

Rather than receiving dignitaries, in May 1961 he became the first president of the United States to speak to the French diplomatic press corps, at a luncheon held at the Palais de Chaillot, to which he arrived very late. He was nervous and ill-at-ease, drinking three glasses of champagne in quick succession, and in acute pain because of a back injury dating from the war. Those standing close enough could see how his hands trembled, even as they gripped the lectern in front of him. The moment he began to speak was the moment he won the audience over. 'Allow me to introduce myself: I'm the guy who Jacqueline Kennedy has brought with her to Paris.' This produced loud applause. He was eagerly listened to. When questions were invited his replies were on the ball. As we left we were each, nevertheless, wondering how this young leader would respond if faced with a grave international crisis. Fresh in all of our minds was the Bay of Pigs fiasco. Would he show better judgement and more determination the next time? Krushchev wanted to find out too, which was why he had asked for the meeting in Vienna.

When JFK arrived in the White House it was with relatively optimistic hopes for East-West understanding. The strategy devised by the team he had gathered around him, Harvard's best and brightest for the most part, was to gauge the Soviets' co-operativeness with specific 'tests', such as Laos and the suspension of nuclear testing. But once in the Austrian capital, the new president found himself tête-à-tête with a thundering Jupiter, determined to get his way in Berlin. Krushchev made no attempt to hide his belief that the West lacked the resolve to oppose him. As they took leave of one another, Kennedy remarked, 'It will be a long, cold winter'. The Russian leader did not appear very impressed by this understatement. The Wall went up; the West was seen to waver.

In the ensuing negotiations, the Kremlin sensed that it was close to attaining its goal again. But it was disappointed in this expectation, and Krushchev decided to bring the combination of Cuba and missiles into play, to force the issue.

The highpoint of a man destined to be struck down by a killer came when he pondered with his advisers the options he must choose between. He had the wit to act audaciously, then, having succeeded in this, to hold back from exploiting his position of superiority. This was the week that rules for a practical co-existence were finally laid down including no more recourse to nuclear blackmail, given the balance of terror between the two powers. Subsequently, the two presidents established a direct communication. Most of what passes between them can only be conjectured; so far its tangible fruits have been modest: the hotline, exciting the imagination of thriller enthusiasts; the Moscow Treaty. However different they may have been in every other regard, both men, following this brush with catastrophe that their brinkmanship almost brought about, at least shared the same awareness, as barely anyone else could, of the danger that threatens us all.

It is a profoundly character-developing type of experience. Kennedy was no doubt a gifted and ambitious politician at the moment he assumed the supreme office, having proceeded along the fast route the fates and his favoured background had arranged for him. His language was elegantly staunch. Ted Sorensen's unrivalled penchant for Churchillian resonance was put to the service of his friend's speeches, that are amongst the finest living examples of the American vernacular. Jack Kennedy was easily the most cultured of all the American presidents, who had a more than passing knowledge of men, that came from fighting with them against the Japanese, and the political arena, that could be more vicious still. His epiphany concerning the scale of responsibility with which he had been invested towards the whole of humanity, by a mere majority of 100,000, had yet to come. Those who were there in June to hear his peace speech, in which he renewed the theme of civil rights within the United States, were left in no doubt that he now assumed it. His conviction of this being a high calling was clear from the rawness of his voice, communicating to his fellow Americans the obligation that, from both reason and a common bond, they were all under to those who did not share their beliefs, or live in the same manner as they did, or whose skin was not the same colour as their own.

A straightforward simplicity

Married to a young woman whose family had come from France, the president liked, and had a better understanding of, the country than most of his predecessors. General de Gaulle, who he went to see first on his initial tour of Europe, was happy to recognise his great potential. If the visit was not to be returned during John Kennedy's lifetime, it had nothing to do with de Gaulle wishing it that way. The American president was himself happy to receive representatives from France; even a journalist would find himself being questioned with keen interest for insights into the best way of resuming the dialogue with a man Kennedy genuinely respected, whose way of thinking he seemed to divine.

Sitting at an oblique angle in his rocking chair, its wooden arms in a firm grip, and with protocol almost set aside, he moved gently back and forth, and looked at one frankly. The introduction into the famous Oval Office, with its floor-length windows offering views across the White House lawn, was without fuss or ceremony. This foreigner had difficulty in recognising that he was sitting opposite the leader of the most powerful empire the world has seen. JFK's charm resided in his simplicity of manner, in the art of knowing how to put the other person at ease, as though one had all the time in the world when, in fact, there were twenty different matters that awaited him, all of them equally urgent and demanding. It was soon evident speaking to him that he meant what he said about democracy, America and the rights of man and that, although a calculating politician, his faith in these was not feigned. An outmoded political system and over-mighty lobbies, the cumulative effect of a fifteen-year-old Cold War and the obstacles of prejudice and sectarian pride often constrained him. There were instances of indecision and mistakes were made. As well as success, he had his share of failure. This did not alter the pleasure he took in life and what, power included, it had to offer. John Kennedy showed an amazing ease in shouldering what could be an overwhelming burden. Like us all he had his weaknesses, but he combined qualities of intelligence, character and goodwill that, especially in such an office, are rarely encountered. His assassination was the act of a fool.

Born on 29 May 1917 in the Brookline suburb of Boston (Massachussets), John Fitzgerald Kennedy was elected to the presidency on 20 January 1961. He was assassinated on 22 November 1963 in Dallas (Texas) and ceremoniously buried in Arlington National Cemetery, close to Washington D.C. His presumed assassin, Lee Harvey Oswald was murdered by Jack Ruby. Ruby died during the course of his appeal trial, on 3 January 1967.

Ho Chi Minh

A Personality Requiring No Cult

On 2 September 1945 the Democratic Republic of Vietnam was proclaimed. The struggle against Japanese occupation and French colonialism was led by Ho Chi Minh, who had become a communist when living in France. Thirty years on, Saigon, the South Vietnamese capital, would bear his name. Having met Ho on several occasions, his obituarist relates the episodes of his life.

(1969)

'My past? I don't think you would find it all that interesting. My current activity matters more...' How many times did Ho Chi Minh utter those words so as to discourage any one of us amongst the press who tried to glean or check details of the birth, upbringing and early career of the Democratic Republic of Vietnam's founder?

Although it might seem unlikely, the biography of the only representative of the 'International' still active, the sole member of the 1924-26 Comintern who still plays an important role in world politics, remains full of uncertainties and contradictions.

It is possible for an historian to write a reliable biography of Mao or Togliatti. But who could claim to accurately chart Ho Chi Minh's extraordinary progress across an agitated revolutionary sea until around 1940, when he adopted both the name he will be remembered by and the persona of a Marxist Gandhi?

What is at least known is that he was born at Kiem-Lien, a little village in Nghé-An province (North Annam, close to Vinh). The landscape, divided by bamboo hedges and dotted with mulberry trees, has a stifling feeling. Behind are the pink-hued mountains; far away in the distance the murmuring sea can be heard. It is poor countryside, unable to support a dense population.

So much for his place of birth. The date may be taken as 19 May 1890, although half the written accounts suggest 1892. He came from a poor family. His father, Nguyen Sinh Huy, received a modest education and worked as a clerk. (…)

Aged 20, with his studies at Hué University still unfinished, he was engaged as a cabin boy on the *Latouche-Treville*, shortly before it made the passage to France. Here, he worked for a while, following his arrival, as an under-gardener. Staying in Le Havre he adopted the *nom de guerre* Nguyen Al Quoc (Nguyen the patriot). He then made his way to Great Britain. He remained there when war broke out, finding work as a road sweeper and in a restaurant. There was a brief visit to the United States, after which he started reading his way through popular Marxist literature, then appearing for the first time.

From Nguyen al Quoc to Uncle Ho

He arrived in Paris in 1917. With hindsight the story of 'Mr Ho comes to Paris' is amongst the most important and laden with significance of the early twentieth-century. Living in down-at-heel lodgings in the rue Marché-aux-Patriarches, then at Marcadet, he was the founder and director, editor and cartoonist of the anti-colonialist paper *Pariah*, which recognised the first Algerian nationalists. Quoc's meetings were known to the police and the tracts were distributed clandestinely. He wrote articles for *La Vie Ouvrière* (*The Working Class Condition*) and *Le Populaire*, as well as being a propagandist in anti-military campaigns. As a member of the Socialist Party the thirty-year-old, but young and sickly-looking man, made a heartfelt appeal for the freedom of colonial peoples at the Congress of Tours, where he aligned himself with the Cachin/Vaillant-Couturier faction. He was now a communist – as he would remain for the rest of his life – vowing to serve the liberation struggle of the world's workers, the 'real' proletariat, coloured men. Above all, the Vietnamese.

Most who knew him at the time recall his charm and palpable sensitiveness and an excessive manner. His room-mate, Trimh, protested that he had difficulty getting sleep. Throughout the night Quoc would talk, smoking one cigarette after another, of socialism's future, freedom for the oppressed, of sublime Vietnam. It was in this fomented after-hours atmosphere that he composed the pamphlet *Trial and Condemnation of French Colonialism*, helped by another of his intimates, Nguyen Thé Truyen. It would be reiterated, virtually word-for-word, by the revolutionary government in Hanoi's first proclamation on 2 September 1945.

Quoc's arrival in the Soviet Union at the beginning of 1924 coincided with Lenin's death. He assumed a role within the leadership of Kresintern, the Peasant International, before moving on to the Comintern. In her book *From Lenin to Mao*, Ruth Fischer, a German comrade, gave a portrait of Nguyen Al

Quoc in his Moscow period: shy, but friendly in a straightforward way, a little naive perhaps, and considered by other leaders of the Third International to be sensitive and clever, if not a master of theory.

His next stop, the eighteen months of education and conference attendance in Moscow concluded, was China. His role was now interpreter-cum-adviser for Borodin, the Comintern delegate – so Malraux's future hero made the acquaintance of the future Mr Ho, now starting to assert his authority. The Vietnamese exiles grouped around him; the Le Than Nienh, or Youth Party was founded. A weekly paper was soon propounding its doctrine, more nationalist than Marxist. The name, nevertheless, of the party he was creating with his two most loyal supporters, Hong Son and Hô Tung Mau, was the Indochinese Communist Party (ICP). Three years would pass before it was formally created on 3 February 1930. (…)

As orchestrator of the troubles in Nghé-An, Quoc was sentenced to death *in absentia*. The French police unsuccessfully sought his extradition, following his arrest by the British authorities in Hong Kong. (…)

During the Popular Front period the ICP operated legally and he assumed a background role: while his key followers, Pham Van Dong, Vo Nguyen Giap and Tran Van Giau, created newspapers and moved amongst the people, his death sentence prevented him from returning to Indochina.[1] But, once the party was proscribed, in 1939, Nguyen Al Quoc forthrightly resumed its leadership. This was most transparent at the Tsin-Tsi Congress of 10-19 May 1941 in southern China, which brought together most of the Vietnamese communist leaders. An upshot was the drawing up of a manifesto that was to remain the Viet Minh's (League for the Independence of Vietnam) reference point.

This new league immediately found itself drawn into, sometimes surreal, talks with the Chinese authorities, eager for its help against the Japanese (already in Indochina), but fearful of the potential development of a Communist cell in Kouang Si or Yunnam. The main prompt for Nguyen Al Quoc's change of name was to set – at least nominally – his relations with the Kuomintang straight. Until then his file was classed among 'dangerous communist agitators'. His new name was to be Ho Chi Minh, 'he who sheds light'.

1945: the way is clear

The great adventure now began. Ho Chi Minh and his followers made their way into Indochina, choosing Thai-Nguyen as their capital. They established a foothold here, incited sedition in the garrison and spread out into Cao-Bang, Lang-Son and Bac-Kan provinces. Deciding the time had come to act, Vichy planned to move against the Viet Minh on 10 March 1945. In a twist of fate, Ho Chi Minh and his followers were to be saved by the Japanese – on the 9th the French forces found themselves hemmed in by the Japanese army. The fates had favoured Ho Chi Minh.

The collapse of the French forces not only saved the Viet Minh leaders in the short term – it handed them the keys to power. The Japanese army was not as capable of being an effective bulwark against a revolutionary movement as the colonial administration. It remained a danger however; or would have, if Ho Chi Minh had not been propelled to power by Hiroshima. Four days later he gave the order for a general insurrection. Japan had been knocked down and the French presence was flattened in the process. The two adversaries had been killed off together, leaving the way clear.

On 2 September, Independence and the Republic were proclaimed simultaneously. Hanoi residents learned that the president was a certain Ho Chi Minh. Their baffled reaction was: 'Who?' The better informed were able to provide the name Nguyen Al Quoc. 'Ah! Yes. The Communist leader.' (...) It took scarcely a month before he was established as leader, with the attention of almost the whole population.

An unseen and, more specifically, noiseless entrance: in the colonial governor's ample office, where foreign visitors are received, his sandals glide across the parquet floor. The voice is slight, carrying the trace of a lisp, and is accented a little, though it is hard to say how – maybe Chinese or, possibly, English. But the man ... creates an immediate impression that will not be forgotten, with a remarkably rare, burning look beneath bushy eyebrows, expansive brow and sparser hair, that is a thing of spiky tufts. He would look a little comic, were it not for the dignity imbuing his profile and face.

Sitting on the edge of the well-upholstered sofa, his feet neatly tucked in together, he speaks both airily and with irony, gesturing with his hands: 'A people like the French, who have benefited the world by a literature that is infused with the spirit of liberty, will always have a friend in us, whatever may come to pass; you ought to know, Monsieur, the enthusiasm with which I reread Victor Hugo and Michelet every year.[2] I can sense that they are the unaffected voice of your popular classes, who share some strange connection with our own people. Ah! Monsieur, what a terrible force colonialism must be to affect men as it does.'

Dressed in a worn, sandy-coloured tunic, not unlike those of Stalin, or colonial pensioners' who have retired to Provençal fishing villages, Mr Ho puts one in mind of a venerable scholar of the Manchu dynasty, reincarnated this time in the uniform of the revolution.

I would see him again. The first time, within a few weeks, was in the company of General Leclerc; on the second occasion, that came a few months later, I was with Admiral Argenlieu.[3] It was something of a mystery how Leclerc, with his well-earned reputation for both integrity and as an uncompromisingly patriotic military leader, got on so cordially, even jovially, with the subtle old communist leader who greeted him on the porch at Government House. When Admiral Argenlieu met the president in Cam-Ranh bay, in the wake of Mr Ho's attendance at the Fontainebleau Conference, the occasion was less cordial, though still courteous.[4] Their talks aboard the cruiser *Suffren* lasted three hours, at which point the three journalists present were drawn into the conversation. Ho called upon us to 'play our part in constraining people's ardour'. Turning promptly to the astonished admiral, he expressed his respectful sentiments...

This was characteristic of the way he presented himself to the world and, above all, to his own people as 'Uncle Ho', a cool, gentle and simple leader with a direct gaze and eyebrows that lifted in astonishment. Vietnamese children would be treated to the oranges and sweets that this St Francis of Assisi of the underground resistance carried with him, as he walked about in sandals whose soles were worn and a tunic that had seen many years of service. The inside of his coat served to wipe the corners of his mouth; a mat on the floor was his bed.

Poverty in power in Asia could be picturesque …

Situated between Moscow and Peking

Glossing over his role in the 19 December 1946 repudiation of accords he had signed on 6 March with M Sainteny, we find Ho Chi Minh at the start of 1947 as a resistance leader once more.

He again took up the outlaw's existence, one of movement between highland caves, domed hideouts in Thai-Nguyen constructed of branches, and long night-marches. This time though the revolution was less an idea and more an instrument that could be used to secure his goal; he had weapons, provided by both Russian and Chinese allies, and in Vo Nguyen Giap he possessed a gifted strategist, who, with Pham Van Dong, had for ten years been one of his two closest partisans.

From the guerilla warfare of 1947 to the first actual battles of 1950, Giap's divisions gained the experience they were then able to use to devastating effect at Dien Bien Phu. Consequently, at the Geneva Conference on 21 July 1954 an independent Vietnam came into being for the second time. The dire economic situation however, in the truncated northern section granted to the victors, dictated a policy of socialist austerity.

The gardener's cottage in the grounds of the former French governor's mansion was where the old man, invariably dressed in his sandy tunic, chose to resume his charting of the Vietnamese revolution's course. It was not always easy to navigate between Moscow – to which he still seemed to be attached by revolutionary ties of both the head and the heart – and Peking, the powerful neighbour; but his watchword remained: Vietnam!

The next time that I met him was towards the end of 1962, faithful Pham Van Dong by his side. The wispy negotiator of 1946 was now, in his old age, almost infant-like in appearance, a rosy-cheeked grandfather of permanent revolution. His charm was intact and he still had a talent for fun and friendliness, with repartee and a taste for paradox continuing to come easily to him. He noted, for example, that 'it is interesting to see that the rebel, de Gaulle occupies the Élysée whilst exile awaits Salan, the establishment conformist'.[5]

Born on 19 May 1890 near Vinh (North Annam), Ho Chi Minh died in Hanoi on 3 September 1969.

Tito

The Man Who Never Fell in Line

When he died in 1980, his obituary ran to three pages. The Yugoslavian president was not just the last surviving anti-Nazi leader, but the one who had dared to stand up to the Soviet Union. Furthermore, his influence was key in founding the non-aligned movement. With Tito gone, his obituarist posed the question: who remains to inspire the respect of even the bitterest enemy?

(1980)

Before age and glasses intervened, it was the steel-like eyes that made an immediate, striking effect. 'A pair of daggers,' said one Bulgarian, who encountered him on a number of occasions; in counterpoint to a face that was growing fleshy and a too-studied care of how he looked – the nouveau riche elegance – his piercing regard served as a reminder of the kind of struggle and adversary that this man had taken on.

His real name was Josip Broz. Before the war he was more commonly known within the Communist International by the pseudonym 'Walter', until in 1937 he traded this alias in for that of 'Tito', the name by which he would become celebrated. When the two syllables first began to make themselves heard during the war, they provoked some eccentric rumours. There were those who claimed that TITO stood for 'Third International Terrorist Organisation', while a leading American broadsheet went so far one day as to suggest that it signified a woman.

It would be hard, however, to imagine a more virile specimen than the infant born to a Croatian father and Slovenian mother in Kumrovec, Croatia in May 1892. He was the seventh child of fifteen. Seven was also the number that survived to adulthood. (…) The father drowned his sorrows in alcohol and it was left to the mother to keep the family afloat. They frequently had no bread to eat. Josip though had the chance to go to school. He was an outstanding pupil in divinity and gymnastics until his studies ended at the age of twelve, when he was apprenticed to a locksmith. It did not take long for him to be drawn into the drama of the workers' struggle and, aged eighteen, he joined the Social Democrat Party of Croatia and Slovenia. His political activity took him from one factory to the next across Central Europe. As he went he learned German and Czech.

The war arrived. Called up as under-officer in the Austro-Hungarian army he was seriously wounded while serving in the Carpathians. As a prisoner, he was lucky to escape being killed by Adyghe before being transferred to a POW camp in the Urals.[1] Here it was typhus that he might have succumbed to. Instead he learned Russian and developed Bolshevik contacts. Although enrolled in the Red Guard, Tito did not see action during the October Revolution. He was passing time in Ekaterinburg (now Sverdlosk) when the anti-Bolshevik Admiral Kolchak gained control of the city with Czech forces. Kirghiz peasants helped him to hide; then he carried on his way. Many adventures and several jail cells were encountered before his return to Croatia in September 1920. With him was the young Russian bride he had married in Omsk, who soon afterwards gave birth, but the baby died within forty-eight hours. They would have three more children, one of whom survived. Josip Broz found work in a mechanic's workshop in Zagreb and joined the Communist Party. When it won fifty-eight seats in parliamentary elections that year, the government's reaction was to ban its propaganda activity. Twelve months later it outlawed the party. (...) Tito was once again on the move, working in a succession of towns across Croatia and taking an active part in the CPY's (Communist Party of Yugoslavia) clandestine network. In 1928 this earned him five years' hard labour. He came across his old comrade Mosha Pijade once more. Pijade, who had been arrested before him, would become one of his most trusted followers.

At the same time that he was in prison, on 6 January 1929, King Alexander abolished the constitution and established his own dictatorship. All political parties were proscribed.

When he was released in 1934, Tito set off incognito to the USSR. He worked for the Balkans section of the Comintern, where he got to know the Bulgarian Dimitrov. Following a secret mission recruiting volunteers for Spain, it was largely thanks to his friend's recommendation that he was designated head of the CPY in 1937. The Stalinist purges were reaching their crescendo. His Bosnian predecessor, Milan Gorkić was liquidated as a western agent. As he had done with the Polish party – having been subsumed under the Comintern, its leaders were summoned to the Kremlin and the majority summarily executed – so the Soviet leader was on the verge of dispensing with the CPY. Finally, he satisfied himself by disbanding its central committee. According to rumours, that have never been officially confirmed, he may nevertheless have been contemplating Tito's removal. It is also likely that the Yugoslavian owed his life to Dimitrov, who warned him in time, permitting a narrow escape.

At the same time that he was making trips abroad to organise volunteers for republican Spain, most frequently in France, Tito, unlike Gorkić before him, took the decision to establish the Communist Party illegally within Yugoslavia itself. Its thoroughgoing reorganisation was intended to bring an end to factional competition and to assure its financial independence from the Kremlin. When war broke out the party had twelve thousand members, its youth affiliation thirty thousand.

The uprising

Being disciplined members of the Comintern, the CPY delegation supported the Nazi-Soviet pact. It had greater difficulty explaining, to its members and to itself, the Yugoslavian ambassador's expulsion from Moscow in April 1941. The reason given was that, in spite of Stalin having signed an *entente* with Belgrade a few days before (intended to help it stand up to Hitler's pressure), with the Royal Army's defeat the country had ceased to exist.

At the end of April, the CPY's central committee, meeting secretly in Zagreb under Tito's presidency, took the precautionary measure of building up a cache of weapons that might be used in a future uprising. The preparations were far enough advanced when the Germans attacked the USSR on 22 June 1941 for the signal to be given.

Within three months the 'Partisans' and Tito their commander-in-chief were already in control of large areas of the country. Part of Serbia was taken by another resistance grouping, the 'Chetniks'. Led by General Mihailović it consisted mainly of

Royal Army soldiers who had evaded capture. They tended to be Serbians, whose aim was to maintain the monarchy and their nation's pre-eminent role. But the future state which Tito and his supporters dreamt of was not likely to be a welcoming one for a royalist and nationalist of Mihailović's kind. The split was not long in coming. As in Greece and Poland, two rival resistance groups would be involved in skirmishes with one another.

A June 1943 report, drawn up at Churchill's request by the War Ministry, came to the clear conclusion that it was the Partisans who were genuinely waging war against the Nazis. So as to have this confirmed or denied, the prime minister sent out a liaison mission, led by the young Conservative MP Fitzroy Maclean. The Partisans' romantic allure and courage made a strong impression on Maclean, for whom they combined the spirited ferocity of the old *comitadji* with cold Bolshevik determination.[2] Back in London, he convinced the government to withdraw its support from Mihailović, and to send a permanent liaison mission to the Partisans' HQ in Bosnia. This would include Randolph Churchill, the prime minister's son. Churchill himself, when the 'Big Three' met in Tehran for the first of their wartime summits in November 1943, prompted Roosevelt and Stalin to recognise Tito.

Because up to that point the USSR, in spite of repeated requests, had been wary of giving the slightest assistance to the Partisans' leader, soon promoted to marshal by AVNOJ (Anti-Fascist Council of National Liberation of Yugoslavia). Maintaining diplomatic relations with the royal government-in-exile, it had proposed its own liaison mission to Mihailović. The Georgian's motives are now understood, but at the time they were not. In the first place he did not want to disconcert his 'bourgeois' allies, by appearing to favour the Communist Party too strongly. During the Spanish Civil War he had displayed the same caution. A separate reason was that, as he turned his thoughts to the future division of Europe, he saw Yugoslavia as a bargaining counter that he would concede to Churchill. He did not want a country within Moscow's sphere of influence that was not actually under it and which, he did not doubt, would pursue its own policies. (...) It was agreed at Tehran to try and bring the royal government and the Partisans closer together, while leaving Mihailović to his fate. In June, Tito went to the Adriatic island of Vis for talks with Šubašić, the Ban of Croatia, whom Churchill had obliged Peter II to name prime minister. Together they issued an appeal calling on the entire Yugoslavian population to enlist in the Popular Liberation Army.

The Germans' recent general offensive had left this force in a precarious state. Tito himself had come close to capture by parachutists who, on 25 May, made a raid on his Drvar HQ. It was only by hiding in a cave, and sacrificing his marshal's uniform to them, that he managed to evade the enemy.

A conversation with Stalin

Šubašić and Tito had an agreement not to anticipate the question of the post-war regime. (...) Without mentioning the trip, Tito flew to Moscow in mid-May 1945. Stalin tried to persuade him to agree to a royalist restoration. 'Not for ever, of course,' he explained, 'just for the time being and then, as soon as you have the opportunity, stab him from behind'. This kind of conversation did not coincide with the western view, which assumed Tito to be Stalin's proconsul-designate for Yugoslavia.

The Soviet leader's caution came into play again when the Belgrade government, in which Tito had complete control over the non-communist members, adopted a frequently provocative attitude to the Allies, now that liberation and victory had been attained. For example, a quasi-ultimatum from the Allied Military Authority was required to stop the annexation of Trieste and the surrounding Friuli-Venezia Giulia region. It was Stalin who advised Tito – now president of the Republic of Yugoslavia, after the parliament elected in autumn 1945 had deposed the king – to back down.

Tito's posture when he staked claims was not a vaunting one, and generally suggested that he was merely the loyal administrator of Soviet policy. In several instances though the Soviet Union, suspicious of its confident pupil's initiatives, sought to dampen their effects. This was the case with both Mihailović's death sentence and the bringing to trial of the archbishop of Zagreb, Mgr Stepinać, who had collaborated with Croatia's separatist leaders during the occupation. In this context, there were very few for whom the 1948 denunciation of the CPY's deviationism, and its expulsion from the Cominform, did not come as a total surprise. (…)

Moscow had treated Yugoslavia as though it were conquered territory, dictating the, slower, tempo at which it considered Tito's collectivising should be undertaken, seeking to take effective control of its economy via government-owned corporations, and recruiting agents for its secret services. Stalin also envied the Yugoslavian marshal his popularity. Tito's heroic stand during the war assured his triumphal reception in all the European capitals.

Even though Stalin agreed with it in principle, Tito's independent proposal of a true 'Land of the South Slavs' with Bulgaria could not be allowed. Before and after all: 'divide and rule'.

'Trotsky-fascist agent'

Since Belgrade would not give in to the blackmail, that he would not renew their economic accords, on 28 June 1948 Stalin moved to strike a decisive blow. With his customary scorn for the 'minor' states, he was convinced that he could dispose of Tito with a flick of his finger, as Krushchev revealed at the Twentieth Congress of the CPSU (Communist Party of the Soviet Union). The Communist Parties' representatives within the Cominform declared that the CPY had adopted a 'false line', that it had defamed the USSR, and was maintaining a 'wholly despotic and terrorist' regime. 'Sound elements' from within the CPY were invited to make its leaders either recognise their mistakes or to step down.

But when a group of Yugoslav Stalinists set about organising a coup in July, the affair barely got off the ground; two of the plotters, Zujović and Hebrang, were in jail. Tito's policy was approved by the Party's Fifth Congress on 21 July. Another of the coup's leaders, the former chief of the general staff, Jovanović, was killed trying to flee to Romania.

The Kremlin reacted with a particularly violent calumnification. Economic exchanges virtually ceased, diplomatic ties with the other popular democracies were suspended, and frontier incidents became an everyday occurence. Tito, who for thirty years had risked his life to bring about a communist future, was now derided as a 'vile hyena' and 'Trotsky-fascist'. Throughout the Eastern Bloc, those suspected of sharing his ideas were put on trial.

The result of this constant pressure was the opposite of what the Kremlin intended. Within Yugoslavia much of the population, having shared the privations that went with a rapid (industrialising) transition to socialism, rallied to Tito. The

Marshal himself took a fresh look at the West, which he hardly knew. Until now his attitude towards it had been a mixture of hostility and mistrust.

Stalin's death was bound to change the relationship. Krushchev visited Belgrade to convey his regret at what had been allowed to happen. He claimed that 'the documents which had justified the insults and accusations directed against the Yugoslavian leaders ... had been fabricated by enemies of the people, imperialism's wretched agents, who had worked their way into the Soviet party hierarchy'. This scarcely credible version of events stood little chance of satisfying Tito. He demanded and obtained Krushchev's signature to a declaration proclaiming the ideal of co-operation between all states, regardless of their ideological particularities and, its key principle, the right of each country to decide for itself which path to tread towards socialism.

This document, a time-bomb now ticking within the Stalinist monolith, played an important part the following year in the Polish October revolt and then the Hungarian revolution. Nevertheless, when both the party and the regime were swept aside in Budapest after only a few days, Tito acknowledged that, although in itself it was 'a mistake and something he disapproved of', the Soviet intervention was a lesser evil, in his opinion, than 'chaos, counter-revolution and civil war, a world war'. (...)

In the years that followed there would be highs and lows in Tito's and the Soviet Union's relations. He travelled occasionally to Russia, where he always received a triumphant welcome, the tribute to his great deeds. But, as much as Krushchev and Brezhnev pressed him to, he would not return within the girdle of the communist camp.

He preferred non-alignment. This was the banner under which

he and similarly inclined leaders – Nasser, Nehru, Nkrumah, Suharto – gathered their countries. (…) Paradoxically, his active sympathy for the non-aligned position would bring about a rapprochement with the Soviet Union in 1967. Within weeks of the Greek *coup d'état* carried out by the Colonels' junta, the Six-Day War broke out; it came close to precipitating his friend Nasser's downfall. Tito's reading of these events was that America had set about overturning, one after another, any progressive regime in the region. Without delay, he set off for Moscow to try and persuade the ruling troika to increase Soviet aid to Egypt.[3] The decision to sever relations with Israel was made with his knowledge.

In 1968 the political wind came from a different direction. For those who helped to bring about the Prague Spring a leader who had stood up to Stalin could not fail to be a hero. They did not disguise their appreciation of Tito as a model to follow. As such, he offered Dubček his encouragement in finding a separate path to socialism. He received another triumphal welcome when he visited Czechoslovakia in August. But the ovations had barely died down when the armies of five Warsaw Pact countries set off to quash the taste for liberty that had developed in Dubček's Czechoslovakia. There followed a period of high tension in Moscow-Belgrade relations, accompanied by an increase in military readiness. With time, a more relaxed status quo was achieved, as Tito and Brezhnev exchanged visits. Yugoslavia joined its voice to calls for a Helsinki Conference on Security and Co-operation in Europe.

Signs of separatism

As he grew older, the Marshal was no doubt right to sense that foreign influence was at play in the episodes of unrest which affected one or another of Yugoslavia's six republics. Nor, however, could there be much doubt that, unless the ground had been partially prepared, this kind of intrigue would not have flourished. Nehru, who knew the country well, was fond of describing Yugoslavia as being formed by 'six republics, five nations, four languages, three religions, two alphabets and a single political party. Under Tito it has been formed into a state but not, as yet, a nation'. A nation was ultimately what Tito dreamed of bringing about. (...) Helped from without by detente and from within by an improvement in Yugoslavia's standard of living, certain republics, especially Slovenia and Croatia, enjoyed a renaissance of their particularism, with its implicit separatist potential. In order to overcome this danger the 'President for Life', as he now was, began purging their executive bodies. Protesters were sent to prison by the dozen; the ringleaders were confined separately.

Tito's purges had pre-dated this separatist trend: the break with Stalin led to arrests of Cominform representatives; Milovan Djilas, the long-term favourite and, later, in 1966, Ranković, the all-powerful police chief, had been disgraced. Others – the main example being Koča Popović, the surrealist poet who became the Partisans' chief-of-staff, secretary for war and foreign secretary – in spite of their continuing admiration for the Marshal, criticised some of his choices. Sensing a finicky despotism, they discreetly withdrew. Some of the front-ranking younger generation, like Ribičić and Nikčzić were dispensed with. (...) With growing age, Tito was less able to take criticism. A void started to form around him; he was too jealous of his own authority to designate a successor who might, in his own lifetime, attract support.

The self-management solution

To independence, non-alignment and national unity, Tito added the new goal of workers' self-management. In his view this was the only way by which a socialist regime could evolve into a real democracy, and finally hasten Marx's old prophecy of the withering of the state. As an actual policy it was better suited to some enterprises than others. (Its overall economic success remains hard to judge.) Yugoslavia's strategic importance however was clear. She took advantage of it, benefiting from US as well as USSR aid. The flow of foreign tourists was matched by a strong workers' emigration to the West. Both helped to keep the economy afloat. As for social policy, its results were mixed too. (…)

On the world stage – picking a fight with one of the superpowers when he had barely concluded a spat with the other – one can safely say that, to preserve the independence of Yugoslavia, her unity and particular structures, required a resistant's flair, a determination to succeed, a man of Tito's stature. Himmler, who for obvious reasons never met him, once said: 'This old communist, Josip Broz, is a man of substance, and "Marshal" is no more than he deserves. Once we capture him he is to be killed of course. But what I would not give for a dozen German Titos! Leaders with his nerves and resolve that lead him, even when completely surrounded, to never surrender.' Now that he is gone, who is left to inspire the respect of even the bitterest enemy?

Born in May 1892 in present day Croatia, Marshal Tito died in Ljubljana (Slovenia) on 4 May 1980.

Lech Walesa

The Electrician who Became President

The one-time electrician from Gdansk's Lenin shipyard was elected president of the Polish Republic in 1990. A tendency to offer his free and sometimes muddled views had not altered the Polish people's deep affection for 'Solidarity''s co-founder. The reporter, who followed his rise from close by, tells the story.

(1990)

On a summer's day in August 1984, driving across Gdansk in his minibus and being universally recognised by other drivers and pedestrians, signalling 'V' for victory or blowing kisses, Lech Walesa, both touched and proud, proclaimed without compromise: 'You know that you are driving around with the next president of the Polish Republic?' On that day he was on very lively form, ironically saluting the secret police who tailed him, and joking about the success his celebrity had earned him with the ladies. The remark hung lightly in the air, like a successful jest.

It was six years ago: martial law had been suspended but Poland, nevertheless, felt like a jailhouse. 'Solidarity' was a clandestine organisation. Recently awarded the Nobel Peace

Prize, Lech Walesa, aged forty-one, still reported each day at the Lenin shipyard, where he worked as an electrician. With his wife, Danuta and the seven children they then had – there was to be another – he lived in a high-rise apartment on the oversized Zaspa dormitory estate. If the situation in Poland had settled down and was not moving anywhere, nor was the twenty-four-hour police presence in the downstairs lobby. Danuta found this dead-end ambiance depressing: 'I would rather be undergoing real hardships, out of which one could at least imagine some change was going to come. But now,' she said, 'there is just stagnation.'

When he jumped over the perimeter wall on 14 August 1980 to take charge of the shipyard strike, few could possibly have imagined that this small – and still thin – worker with the moustache was going to bring about an historic upheaval. A veteran of the demonstrations that erupted by the Baltic in December 1970, it was not his first act of defiance against the regime. The electrician's subsequent involvement in the labour force's fight for representation had led to his sacking from the shipyard six years later. The next episodes are well-known: the 'Gdansk Accords', permitting the first independent trade union within the Communist Bloc; the alliance of workers and intellectuals characterising 'Solidarity''s progress; General Jaruzelski's emphatic counterforce. On 13 December 1981 the regime swooped to intern the activists, and martial law was proclaimed.

Walesa, who was held separately from both his supporters and his celebrated counsellors, remained faithful to the cause. When he was released on 14 November 1982 it was with his head held high, to share the sombre experience his countrymen were living through. Occasionally he managed to evade his police observation and to make contact with the underground network, but the majority of his former advisers were still imprisoned. Most of the time there was no choice other than to take decisions by himself, without consulting the union's national board. During 'Solidarity''s legal period his authoritarianism had frequently prompted lively concerns, most notably at the first congress of October 1981; however, with General Jaruzelski as ruler, nobody complained any longer, it being well known that clandestine activity and democracy can have little to do with one another. Walesa assumed the role of decision-maker and, 'Well then, it is democratically decided, by myself...' became a favourite phrase.

He generally employed his authority as a moderating influence. It would be hard to keep a count of the occasions on which the president of 'Solidarity' interposed himself to block those elements getting carried away by events. A tried and tested self-limiting strategy was one he had the necessary authority to impose on the movement. He was capable of dissuading those tempted, under martial law, from launching themselves into futile action. Recently Karol Modzelewski, one of the key figures in 'Solidarity', now a parliamentarian, recalled how, 'from 1980, 'Solidarity''s strategists moved to emphasise Walesa's pre-eminence, convinced as they were that a mass movement of this kind was not capable of appreciating what political reality would otherwise dictate and that therefore they would have to be made to do so by a leader whose position was uncontested. But it is those counsellors who made Walesa's leadership who are now challenging it'.

Within a Warsaw Pact country his position was unique. In Czechoslovakia Havel's support could be numbered in hundreds. In Russia there was Sakharov, whose isolation, he confided to Walesa in Paris in December 1988, was starker still.

Is he a hero or a dictator? In attempting an answer it is

probably worth noting that not many amongst Mr Walesa's current critics were so open in voicing their objections – if indeed they had any – before democracy, entailing political rivalries, brought these to the light of day. They would reply that being a good union leader does not automatically make one a good presidential candidate. But it had been a long while since he had limited himself to this union role, when Walesa declared, at 'Solidarity''s second congress last April, that he would be running for the presidency.

The great leap

When the government decided, in September 1988, to hold talks with the opposition, it was only natural that they should be with Lech Walesa. Given that 'Solidarity' was proscribed, the only question was in what capacity? The then deputy leader of the Communist Party, Jozef Czyrek, said that it was to be 'simply as "Mr Walesa" ' and explained, 'independent of the post he holds, each man has a value, weight, authority and history that make him representative'. Two months later, on 30 November, state television gave the go-ahead to a live debate between the official and unofficial union leaders: Mr Alfred Miodowicz versus the president of 'Solidarity'. Walesa's triumph marked a turning point. Ten days later, for the first time since martial law had been declared, he was given permission to travel to France, where he had been invited by president Mitterrand. His adviser, Professor Geremek – 'without whom I would be blind' – went with him. The welcome he received in Paris, both at the Élysée and from M Laurent Fabius at the Hôtel de Lassay, was similar to that accorded a head of state.

By March 1989 the Round Table Discussions had reached an impasse. Lech Walesa therefore criss-crossed Poland, going from meeting to meeting to convince an increasingly mistrustful population of the negotiations' essentially sound basis. It was time for the great leap: 'semi-democratic' elections in June 1989, the first to be held within the Soviet Bloc. Walesa was on hand to help two hundred and sixty one – with each of whom he had his photo taken – 'Solidarity' parliamentary and Senate candidates get elected in a virtual sweep.

Having been knocked back so emphatically, the regime struggled to recover. Adam Michnik proposed that 'Solidarity' form a government. But how should it set about doing this?

Once more it was Lech Walesa who worked it out and presented his solution as a *fait accompli* to the 'Solidarity' MPs – 'since you are incapable of acting yourselves'. They were predisposed to believe him when he said that he was going to have done with the current coalition government, take over as head of government himself and, giving him a night to consider, ask Tadeusz Mazowiecki to be his prime minister. In the words of his adviser, Andrzej Micewski, 'It was his political intuition, his sense that the USSR was coming asunder, that permitted Walesa to see this could be done. The élite did not grasp it; he, the electrician, did.'

However, if a new life suggested itself, he was still just a union leader; it was his former advisers who now occupied the spotlight in Warsaw's political village. For Walesa the period of transition was problematic.

But could anyone who really knew him imagine that, having given so much of himself, he would quietly leave the scene? A 'Solidarity' leader, Wladyslaw Frasyniuk, interviewed by *Gazeta Wyborcza* in January 1990, predicted that, 'Poland will have a new president in the course of the year. His name is Walesa'.

When the presidential elections arrived however, Frasyniuk

campaigned on behalf of Tadeusz Mazowiecki rather than Lech Walesa. In the interim Walesa had caused a split in 'Solidarity' by his decision to 'accelerate' – the word became his leitmotiv – the changes taking place in Poland. His intuition was that impatience and resentment had started to take hold of the population. His opponents said that he could not wait to fulfil his presidential ambitions.

His famous political intuition also told him that, with the government seemingly scuppered in January 1990, now was the time to act and do away with the old regime, once and for all, bag and baggage. Tadeusz Mazowiecki and his advisers were apprehensive; they forecast a breakdown in order. The split between the two friends had been announced; both were profoundly hurt by the exchanges they now shared.

A double-edged sword

Walesa could call upon his close relation with the people. This tried and tested formula never failed him and he was more acute than the Warsaw élite were to the frustration of 'real' Poles. It was something of a double-edged sword though: as well as rallying weary, disoriented Poland he risked unleashing resentment and bitterness, anger and the lure of demagogy.

He talked too much and often in a muddled fashion, proposing contradictory economic reforms. His position on anti-Semitism was less than clear; he attacked the intellectuals. Apart from the majority of this class however, Poles did not hold this against him; they knew and liked him. 'Some of what he says might be a little idiotic,' concedes one of his advisers, 'but not what he does.' In the eyes of western observers the campaign diminished his lustre. They felt more affinity with the political style of Mr Mazowiecki. A difficult year was crowned by the success of Stanislaw Tyminski in the first round of voting on 28 November.

On this occasion Lech Walesa's legendary political acumen was not in evidence: he did not anticipate the Tyminski phenomenon. At the end of round one he was like a boxer seeing stars. Then, in the two weeks that were allotted till the second, he managed to learn the lessons of this humiliating setback. On 9 December he was the winner. Twenty years of struggles, in which he had managed to avoid all the pitfalls and the waylaying influences that were waiting for him, were concluded with his election as Poland's leader by universal suffrage.

But maybe the hardest part was yet to come.

Lech Walesa was born on 29 September 1943 in Popowo, Poland. At the end of his mandate in November 1995 he sought re-election, but was defeated by Aleksander Kwaskiewski, the Social Democrat Party candidate. Standing again in 2000 he received only 1.01% of votes and announced his retirement from politics.

Anatoli Karpov

Chess' Apparatchik

A pure product of the Soviet regime, Anatoli Karpov has found himself unloved in the world of chess. He receives a rough ride from the media on account of his apparatchik personality, while the public reserves its enthusiasm for the charismatic Kasparov or Bobby Fischer's genius. But he is a grandmaster possessed of an unblemished style. For ten years he was world champion.

(1998)

No! Is that really Anatoli Karpov? The badly dressed, apparently insignificant man with lank hair, who can be seen flitting between the Paris' 'Plaza Athénée''s lounges, is the bearer of a champion's name that evokes the intriguing game of chess across the world? The initial impression he makes is confirmed in the course of an interview. With his waxy skin and globular eyes, he reminds one of a fish, or perhaps a toad. At the slightest opportunity the Russian lets loose, in a faintly bitter voice, the antagonism he reserves for his sworn enemy, Garry Kasparov. He maintains his defensive front for two hours. If a question bothers him in some way Karpov will wriggle away, eel-like, on a tangent. If necessary, he rewrites history, with little regard for others' reputations; or he will criss-cross behind his lines, nursing a position in the same way as Nabokov's Luzhin, who organised his life as though he were playing chess: unloved, and on the defensive.

Irrespective of what he does, Karpov will forever remain the apparatchik, branded with the mark of a deeply unpopular regime, the hammer and the sickle. Millions are waiting for him to lose – the anti-charismatic par excellence, the bad guy in the film. When asked about his friends, he replies with a half-smile: 'Naming those I am enemies with would be much easier.'

This is the charge sheet, and something is not quite right about it: if one allows that a face can be deciphered, there is an ironic trace hanging suspended from his piercing grey-green eyes. An inference may also be drawn from the facts that he has been world champion for ten years and, with a near perfect game, the all-time record holder for tournaments won: he cannot be a total wretch. Did you know that for several years he has been in charge of a charity helping veterans of the Second World War, or that recently he has set up another charity, whose work in seventeen countries is to help young musicians, at the same time that he lends a guiding hand to the Junior Chess Olympiad? The Russian player, Valeri Salov, put the paradox in a sentence when he said, 'Karpov is an insoluble equation, an enigma, a mystery'. This is as true of his chess game as his everyday life.

Behind Karpov's well-maintained defensiveness lies Anatoli, 'Tolia' to his friends. At the time that the ex-champion Mikhail Botvinnik unveiled him in 1964, he was a scrawny thirteen-year-old boy. Nicolas Giffard explains in *Guide des Échecs* (*Guide to Chess*) how the adolescent son of a metal worker was then nurtured under the strict regime of a 'Made in the Soviet

Union' test-tube champion. Now began the irresistible rise of this passive lad towards the final goal, and fief of Soviet players since the war: the world title. He was junior champion of Europe in 1967-68 and of the world in 1969. The next year he became an International Grandmaster ... if everything went according to schedule then Anatoli could expect to be crowned with laurels in 1978.

That was before the dramatic events in Reykjavik. In 1972 the eccentric and rough-mannered Bobby Fischer relieved Boris Spassky and the USSR of the supreme title, in convincing style. Deprived by an American of one of its favourite propaganda weapons, the Kremlin was determined to do whatever was necessary to regain it at the earliest opportunity. Karpov's recent results allowed him to ease up the rankings and into the challengers' circle sooner than planned. In a series of eliminating matches, held in Moscow in 1974, his progress was scarcely remarked, until he was contesting the final with Victor Korchnoi, twenty years his senior.

Their pairing brought two opposites together over the chessboard. On one side, a twenty-three-year-old whose dazzling ascent and purified style made an idol; on the other, an aggressive but ageing individualist – not the aseptic ideal the Soviets wished to convey of themselves. Korchnoi later remarked how, 'during the match, Karpov received favourable treatment because he was a blond Russian from the Urals and his family were workers. My sin was not to have fair skin, to be a Jewish history graduate, a bourgeois. They gave me a second-rate team who leaked my game plans...' A lively hatred took hold during their twenty-four games. In the end, Karpov narrowly won the right to challenge 'king' Bobby Fischer. Their encounter, however, was not to be. When the World Chess Federation (FIDE) refused to accommodate all of his random, excessive demands, the American simply ceded his title to Karpov. The affair was none of his doing; nevertheless, it left an indelible stain on Anatoli's reputation.

He now tried to efface it, and prove that he was not champion in name alone. The three-year wait for his title defence was spent in a never-ending procession of tournaments, an opportunity to refine a fearsome, boa-constrictor style of play that made a number of his opponents tremble. He had now mastered the art of constructing a win out of the slightest advantages, grinding away patiently at the task in hand, until it succumbed to his will. 'Karpov is like a spider. He weaves a web around his enemy until there is no escape,' acknowledged Boris Spassky. Not that one would have recognised from his sickly appearance – 6'1" high and only 8st 9lb – the killer instinct the reserved young man hid. At the chessboard he showed scarcely any emotion; only intensity in his survey of its squares to detect a pattern, weakness or deadly trap. The complete opposite of the telegenic show about to be provided by the gesticulating and exuberant Kasparov.

The second blemish

Monsoon rains hemmed in the Philippines' Baguio City convention centre, venue for the world title contest between Karpov and Korchnoi. This far-away country was to play host to the most passionate chess duel of all time, lasting three months from July 1978, and giving rise to episodes of spying and nervous breakdown. *Dangerous Moves*, Richard Dembo's celebrated 1984 film, was largely based upon it.

There had been developments since the 1974 match. During a tournament held in Amsterdam in July 1976, Korchnoi had walked into a consulate to claim political asylum. As an exiled dissident, many came to regard him as the 'Solzhenitsyn of chess', but in the Soviet Union, where his wife and son were forced to remain, he was widely portrayed as a turncoat, and stripped of his nationality. The scene was thus set for Korchnoi v Karpov: the inheritor of Fischer's mantle of liberty, craving revenge versus an inhuman regime and its representative.

In Karpov's corner was a 'Dr' Zoukhar, playing the role of the Soviet champion's supporter. Opposite, Korchnoi's conviction grew that he was a hypnotist, intent on dragging him down. So did Karpov's instant lead until Korchnoi, incredibly, made his way back into the game. It was 5-5. The winner would be the first to win six games. Weighing 7st 5lb, Karpov had taken a bad beating. This physical slightness had been a drawback throughout his career. Korchnoi could apparently go in for the kill. But now it was the champion's turn to surprise. He rallied and held the title.

Korchnoi mounted another challenge in 1981 but his hour had passed. The true challenge for Karpov now came from a magnetic newcomer whose flamboyance left few followers of the game indifferent. He may have been another product of the Botvinnik regime and a member of the CPSU, but the genial enthusiasm of this young man from Azerbaijan, Jewish on one side and Armenian on the other, made him adaptable to the media, as Karpov was not. Anatoli was hardly forthcoming with journalists and had only ever been able to define himself defensively, in terms of others. When Kasparov presented himself as the anti-Karpov, his forthrightness and general aura prevailed. He was accepted as a chess-playing proto-Gorbachev. A white knight.

On 10 September 1984 the first of their five finals commenced. The impetuous youth surged forward – and was repelled by an experienced defence. Playing flawlessly, Karpov gobbled up the 'Baku Ogre', to build a 5-0 lead. Kasparov, in the face of defeat, realised that he had to calm himself. Patiently he waited and, in the weeks that followed, he gained a series of draws. Finally he secured a first game. After this another series of draws. Knocked off-balance, the ageing Karpov was no longer able to endure this type of test. He shed weight, was worn out, experienced difficulty sleeping. This shadow of a former self could no longer decide the best moves to make and lost a sequence of two games. The then president of FIDE, Florencio Campomanes, a Filipino, was prompted – most likely it seems by the Soviet Chess Federation – to intervene in the debacle. The resulting communiqué said neither Russian was winner nor loser, a verdict at odds with that of the entire western press, for whom Kasparov was now champion. As for Karpov, a second blot on his public image and reputation was added to the original acquisition of the title by default. Again, he had not asked for anything; nevertheless, the system had saved him. These days he offers a strangely inventive version of events. 'I was told, once we had been playing for four months that they wanted to make scientific tests on my brain. The results they got after attaching electrodes to it were enough for them to conclude I should stop playing the match. They passed the evidence on to Campomanes saying that, unless he stopped the match, he was going to be responsible for the deaths of the two best players in the world.' The 'they' Karpov refers to would include an Azeri, Guidar Aliev, the FIDE Council's senior vice-president at the time and Kasparov's protector. But what interest did Kasparov have in bringing to an end a match he had just drawn level in? Karpov remains silent. When the other player is asked about this scenario he says, 'Let him live with his illusions'.

'I have the complete collection of chess stamps'

In 1985 the 'Baku Ogre' did win the world championship. Karpov now played second fiddle. For some he simply had the misfortune to be around at the same moment as the greatest player of all time. His, candid, appraisal is slightly different. 'Maybe it was because I had a strong rival that I continued to play at the top for so long.' When Kasparov decided to turn his back on FIDE in 1993 and set up his own chess association, Karpov had little trouble in regaining the cut-price title. He still holds it, and remains a substitute world champion.

Another black mark for his CV. But he does not spend too much time worrying about that; currently he is busy contesting, with the President of FIDE, the latter's reluctance to organise annual challenges for his title. In spite of the USSR's dissolution, down chess' corridors of power nothing seems to have changed: the struggles continue. Karpov, who has filled out to 11st 5lb, rests on his laurels. He does not work like he used to and loses tournaments. He no longer inspires fear.

Today it is his career's side products that occupy him the most and keep him on the move from hotel to hotel, flight after flight. One project is to record a series on the Game of Kings for a Chinese TV channel, for which an aggregate audience of fifteen million viewers is expected! In the meantime this honorary Texan promotes his 'Disney Guide' to chess. Published in sixteen languages, it has already sold in hundreds of thousands. Having been born without a silver spoon in his mouth, he is now becoming wealthy. As for political honours, Brezhnev presented Karpov with the Soviet Union's highest, the Order of Lenin...

The sense of a career's sad recessional is there; stamps is the subject that gets him talking passionately towards the interview's conclusion. 'I have got every single chess stamp. My Olympic Games collection is the fourth or fifth best in the world. I am third or fourth for pre-revolution Russia. For Belgium, a country I like, I am No.1. Next year it will be the one hundred and fiftieth anniversary of the first Belgian stamp. It was issued on 1 July 1849 and I have the first stamp and also one from the first day they were used by the postal service. It is possible to drag me away from chess, you know, for several minutes or, sometimes, hours. Philately is one way.' At this 'Tolia' smiles. His grey-green eyes light up and, in this moment of sincerity, one gets a glimpse of a former innocence.

Anatoli Karpov was born on 23 May 1951 in Zlatooust (USSR). He was eliminated in the first round of the Chess World Championship in 2001. He has since founded chess schools in the CIS (former USSR) and across the world.

Andrei Sakharov

The Dissident Scientist

In 1975, the Nobel Peace Prize was awarded to the Soviet dissident, Andrei Sakharov. A Moscow correspondent's portrait of the famed physicist marked the occasion. 'Father of the Soviet "H" bomb', Sakharov turned into an advocate of arms limitation and, finally, a human rights activist, operating out of an unexceptional Moscow flat, where his campaigns to publicise civil rights violations snowballed.

(1975)

If one is to try and convey Andrei Sakharov's character in as few words as possible, the two that immediately come to mind are 'courage' and 'gentleness'. Such is the impression made on anyone who goes to visit him in the two-room Moscow flat belonging to his mother-in-law, which he has the use of. Tranquil to what appears the point of timidity, into these two cramped rooms the door is open to acquaintances, strangers and foreign journalists alike. It is the centre of his activity: to make known, via a constant protest, each civil rights case that he has been alerted to.

His voice, never raised, scarcely betrays a murmur as he describes the anonymous threats and various bother which different members of his family have been subjected to. Although an obsessive, his eyes' drained blue hue nevertheless suggests sadness more than anger. Such menaces are not about to deflect him from his level-headed and persistent campaigning. Obviously he is aware that, within the Soviet Union, his own case – that of an academician possessing great prestige abroad – is exceptional.

Consideration of his current activity should not permit one to lose sight of Sakharov's background and most essential work, as a scientist of genius. As is often the case with scientists, he came to political consciousness by drawing out the implications of his own work. He was born into a 'bourgeois' Moscow family in 1921. The father was a physics teacher and author of a handful of textbooks, as well as popular science publications. Following his outstanding studies at secondary school, Andrei attended Moscow State University at the age of seventeen. Four years on, rather than dispatching him to the front, the authorities earmarked Sakharov, as an engineer, for service in a munitions factory. He would continue there until the end of the war, already being remarked upon, on account of some early inventions. When hostilities ended he prepared his doctoral thesis under the supervision of Igor Tamm. This renowned physicist was to win the Nobel Prize in 1958.

1948 marked the start of Sakharov's 'nuclear' career. The young Doctor, one of the youngest in the country, was brought into the team creating the 'H' bomb. The sobriquet 'Father of the Soviet "H" bomb,' that is commonly applied to him in the West, is one that he declines to accept. He would rather acknowledge that he provided 'certain key ideas', something of a euphemism according to those qualified to comment. In 1953, year of the

Soviets' first nuclear explosion, Sakharov was elected to the Academy of Sciences. Not only, at the age of thirty-two, was he the youngest academician to date but, exceptionally, he did not have to take the first step of being an associate member.

Krushchev's critic

Sakharov's name came to the notice of Soviet specialists for the first time in 1958, following a *Pravda* article that was critical of a number of Krushchev's proposals for educational reform. He fondly recalls other, more significant, disagreements with Mr K that year. Uneasy at what he considered the cynicism of the 'Military-Industrial Complex"s leadership, as Beria remained in personal control of the nuclear program in 1953, and disturbed not only by the Twentieth Congress's revelations but by the results of his own scientific research, he soon became convinced that the arms race needed limiting. In a letter to Krushchev he recommended that the USSR cancel its upcoming nuclear tests, but to no avail.

Sakharov would return to the subject in 1961; the Berlin crisis' pitch having risen, Krushchev was eager, for reasons of prestige and perception, to stage more tests. At a meeting to which Sakharov and other experts were invited, the scientist passed the Communist leader a new letter, whose essence was that, 'coming after their three-year suspension, a resumption of tests risks jeopardising limitation talks on nuclear tests and missiles'. Krushchev's response came in the form of a public rebuttal, making it clear that whilst he might be a *savant* of the first order, foreign affairs were not his métier. This did not dissuade the academician from taking up the issue once more – and again in vain – when a new test, devoid in his opinion of any scientific purpose, was scheduled in 1962. The following year however saw his point of view triumph, with the signing in Moscow of the Nuclear Test Ban Treaty, that covered both underwater and atmospheric explosions.

Sakharov's overtly political opposition to the regime dates from 1964. At issue this time was Krushchev's nomination of two biologists, both adherents of Lysenko, for the Academy of Sciences.[1] The physicist prevailed, in a contest that also helped in bringing about his friendship with the two brothers, Roy and Jaurès Medvedev. The *samizdat* written by Jaurès, a young biologist himself, on the Lysenko affair was Andrei Sakharov's first encounter with the genre.

Roy Medvedev, meanwhile, was in the middle of writing a history, destined to remain unpublished in the USSR, of Stalinism. As he spent more time in the two's company, so Sakharov's questioning of the Soviet system grew keener. In 1966 he signed a petition addressed to the Twenty-Third Congress of the Communist Party, which called for the process of destalinisation to be taken further. He was also engaged in publicising practical abuses of an important article of the Russian Criminal Code. Drawing out the logic of this position, he spoke up on behalf of four dissidents, or 'free thinkers' as he preferred to call them, who had recently been thrown in jail: Ginzburg, Galanskov, Lachkova and Dobrovolski. Then came the Siniavski-Daniel affair, to which he lent his support.

The academician's crime

It was the foreign publication of *Progress, Coexistence and International Freedom*, in 1968, that brought the scientist to international notice. The book also spelt an irreparable breakdown of his relations with Soviet authority, the regime unsuccessfully trying to exclude him from the Academy. His 'crime' was not to have subscribed to the then current theory of a confluence between capitalist and socialist systems, but to have called instead for an unequivocal letting-go of residual Stalinism, and for a proper respect of what he classed as human rights. Sakharov's position was summarised in a long open letter, addressed to the Soviet authorities in 1970. Co-authored by the Medvedev brothers and the physicist Valentin Turchin, it emphasised the paucity of life which the system imposed on society.

The new decade saw his interventions multiply. He and two other physicists, Andrei Tverdokhebov and Valentin Chalidze, founded the Committee on Human Rights in the USSR. It lent public support to: Jaurès Medvedev who, before his London exile, was placed in an asylum; General Grigorenko, confined in a psychiatric institute, having voiced his dissent against the invasion of Czechoslovakia; the mathematician Pimenov, sent to Siberia for 'defamation of the USSR'; Kuznetsov, a Jew who had been sentenced to death for an attempted plane hijacking, before finally being pardoned; etc.

Andrei Sakharov had also protested Solzhenitsyn's deportation, in spite of his evident opposition to the writer's 'Greater Russian nationalism' and patriarchal, religious posture. In contrast to this other renowned dissident – the protector of 'old' values – the physicist's protest, allowing for its occasional political naivety (regarding Chile for example), was clearly 'modern'.

'It is my belief,' goes a key passage in which he denounces Solzhenitsyn's focus on the past, 'that democracy is the best system for no matter which country. Our centuries-old fascination for slavism, mixing xenophobia with racism and intolerance of minority beliefs, has not been a benefit but a curse for Russia.'

In recent years Sakharov's isolation has grown. Most of his friends are gone, having been imprisoned or entered exile in the West. His work continues, but he preaches, one is obliged to say, in a kind of desert that the authorities have created around him. The second wind given to the dissident scientist by its award is not something the Nobel Committee is about to be forgiven for by the Kremlin.

****

When Andrei Sakharov died in December 1989, the former correspondent paid his respects to the figure who, since 1975, had spent six years' exile in Gorky, before rehabilitation by Mikhail Gorbachev.

(1989)

A true democrat

Some deaths are felt more than others, Andrei Sakharov's being particularly tragic for his country. Stooped and fatigued by the years of protest and humiliation, he remained a rare species in the Soviet Union: a genuine democrat. If Solzhenitsyn was the living soul of Orthodox, pre-Soviet Russia, Sakharov represented the USSR's democratic conscience. Amidst a sea of obscurantism, here was a humanist who, without party in a single-party state, remained free in spirit when fear and brutalisation were the norm, and maintained his integrity in spite of the system's endemic corruption and favouritism, by never renouncing his convictions.

His combat with authority had earned him six years in exile. Returning from Gorky he was a little more bent and weary. His voice had grown fainter still, but he remained as determined as ever.

It would have been easy enough, following his rehabilitation by Mr Gorbachev, for Sakharov to have slipped into a role as guru of a society in transformation. But, knowing his country as he did, he declined to play the part. There would first be the inevitable impasses and obstacles to overcome, traps to be avoided, before any outcome was assured. Harbouring reservations towards both *Glasnost* and *Perestroika* he was not prepared to be their propagandist. His scepticism concerning Gorbachev, whom he assessed without sentimentality, went even deeper. Calmly, he continued to follow an undeviating path towards real democracy, uninterested in cheap victories that might be gained in the reform of a system that could not, ultimately, be reformed. To stop halfway would be to slip back.

Sakharov would remain unbiddable to the end, still contesting with the Soviet authorities, up to and including Gorbachev himself. The last in their series of confrontations took place in the Russian Parliament two days before his death. *À propos* abolishment of the Communist Party's 'leading role' their duel, though it occupied a brief moment, was highly revealing. To one side, an old man of controlled but unshakeable zeal, symbolising the opposition; on the other, the man of power, in a sudden outburst of angry, disdainful authoritarianism. Within seconds their scene was over: it nevertheless deserves studying. The aspect Gorbachev displayed is no less pertinent than those images of his amiable and civilised demeanour which we have grown accustomed to.

Born in Moscow on 21 May 1921, Andrei Sakharov died there on 24 December 1989.

Golda Meïr

'Grandmother' of the Israeli State

Born in Kiev in the Ukraine, Golda Meïr grew up in the United States before deciding to emigrate to Palestine in 1921. She served as Israel's foreign minister, then became prime minister at the age of seventy. She was the third woman in world politics to attain such a post, and was known, long before Margaret Thatcher, as the 'Iron Lady'.

(1978)

Golda Meïr, who was one of its key players, never ceased to lay all the blame for the Israeli-Arab conflict on the adversary. This, frequently over-simplified, analysis of the situation would even lead her at the end of her career to sympathise with the old Likud rival, whose intransigence she admired; if she continued to criticise Menachem Begin, for example in the wake of Camp David, it was because he too was capable of making 'too many concessions'.

She was already seventy at the time her 'second political life' commenced. The compromise choice to succeed Levi Eshkol as prime minister – so as to avoid either extreme in a potential intra-party struggle for power, between Moshe Dayan and Yigal Allom, when Eshkol died in February 1969 – Golda Meïr would subsequently, and against all expectation, remain in office for more than five years. (...)

A conviction politician

The belief that Israel had done everything within her power to bring about a just and honourable peace with the Arabs and that it was they, most particularly Egypt, who impeded such an outcome, lay at the heart of Meïr's position. A February 1971 peace proposal of President Sadat's, that was dependent upon the Occupied Territories restitution, was rejected. In the wake of the Yom Kippur War, she insisted that 'we have done everything we can to achieve peace and do not share any of the blame for this war!' A war that produced a storm within Israel, obliging her to resign. She was made to share responsibility with Moshe Dayan, the principal culprit of *mehdalim*, or oversights, that had invited the attack. Her inflexible line nevertheless remained the same as that stated to *Newsweek* in an April 1969 interview: 'I am not interested in the Jewish people being generous, liberal, anti-colonialist, anti-imperialist – and dead.' Her condemnation of moderates' 'defeatism' was never long in coming. She forestalled their initiatives, for example that of Nahum Goldmann's proposed trip to Cairo in April 1970, wherever she could.

Committed heart and soul to defending the Jewish people's interests, she refused to acknowledge that the Palestinians might possess rights to this land. Following the Six-Day War, when the question was being hotly debated, she went as far as denying the Palestinian people's existence. In a gale of laughter she let it be known: 'Why, I am a Palestinian, too! The British gave me a Palestinian passport under their mandate.'

Born in the Ukrainian capital of Kiev on 3 May 1898 to a family of few means, Golda Meïr endured the harsh experience of her race's pogroms during her childhood. These helped to form an inflexible character. She would later say: 'Because of persecutions and hardships, I never feared the Goyim or felt respect for the rich.' In 1906 the family emigrated to Milwaukee, Wisconsin. Living conditions here were scarcely easier than back in the Ukraine. Golda helped her mother, who had a little grocery store in a part of the town seething with lower-class life. At the age of fifteen she left the family home, to pursue her dream of studying. She earned her living at a laundry. It did not take long before Golda was drawn into politics; by 1915 she was active within Poale Zion (Workers of Zion).

Six years later she emigrated to Palestine, taking the husband she had married at nineteen, Maurice Meyerson, with her. The young couple joined the Merhavia kibbutz, where she enthusiastically raised chickens and worked in the fields; he less so. Not sharing her political convictions, he wanted to return to America. Following three years of the communal life and so as to preserve their home together, she consented to a move to Tel Aviv, where she worked as a laundry woman to supplement the meagre salary he received as an accountant. At the same time Golda remained a committed political activist. In 1925 she became a member of Solel Boneh, the construction firm branch of Histadrut (The General Federation of Labourers). She was then elected secretary, in 1928, of the Women Workers' Council. Four years later she was charged with a twelve-month mission to the United States, where she was named secretary of the Zionist Organisation of Female Pioneers. Her rise within Histadrut culminated in being elected in 1934 to the secretaryship of its executive committee and then to run its political department. A regular participant at Zionist Congresses, she also became a member of the Palestinian Jewish Community's National Committee. Her talents as a speaker and trenchant debater were already evident. (...)

This burgeoning political activity was added to shortly before the state of Israel came into being, when she was entrusted with a number of secret missions. Dressed as an Arab woman, and in the greatest secrecy, she met King Abdullah of Jordan on three occasions, to try and win his commitment not to take part in a war that the Arab countries were preparing to unleash on the newly born state. During the last of their meetings, four days before the Israeli Declaration of Independence, the Hashemite king revealed his astonishment: 'I do not understand why the Jews are in such a rush,' he said, before proposing that the creation of a Jewish state should be postponed to a later date. 'We've been waiting for two thousand years. Is that hurrying?' Mrs Meyerson asked.

Following independence, she went to the USSR with the rank of minister plenipotentiary. Her arrival roused the lively enthusiasm of the Jewish population which, in unrepressed fashion, proclaimed its solidarity with Israel. When she was elected to the first Knesset in 1949, she made her way back to the new country, serving as employment and social security minister until 1956. Her entry into the government created discomposure amongst cabinet members belonging to the religious parties. Their refusal to sit at the same table as a female colleague caused a temporary crisis.

The Ben Gurion bust-up

Whilst the fledgling state of Israel started to gather momentum along a capitalist path, Golda Meyerson remained committed to founding a socialist regime. During the 1 May celebrations of 1950, in a variation of one of the diaspora's favoured cries, she ventured the challenge: 'See you next year in a socialist Israel.'

When she led Mapai's list of candidates to victory in Tel Aviv in the 1955 local elections, the religious parties this time succeeded in preventing her from becoming the city's mayor. Her close allegiance to Ben Gurion, whose hardline foreign policy stance she shared, particularly towards the Arabs, helped her being named foreign minister in succession to Moshe Sharett the following year: his moderate approach had ultimately exasperated the prime minister. Having hebraicised her name (from Meyerson), Meïr presided at the Foreign Ministry until January 1966. The unyielding manner in which she argued her case with foreign diplomats would become well known.

It did not take long however for relations between herself and Israel's founding father to deteriorate. From 1960, the 'Lavon Affair''s fresh eruption, as well as ongoing disputes between the foreign minister and various partisans of the 'Old Lion' holding high ranking posts at the Ministry of Defence, most notably its deputy minister, Shimon Peres, with his tendency to infringe upon her own prerogatives, would continue to push two equally obstinate and powerful personalities apart.[1] Gradually, Meïr started to rival Ben Gurion at the head of Mapai, the Labour Party's predecessor. In 1963, Levi Eshkol's assumption of the premiership strengthened her position and, two years later, she delivered a detailed indictment of her one-time intellectual guide. His schismatic founding of a new party, Rafi, entailed the two leaders' definitive rupture, although a reconciliation would take place in 1970 when, as prime minister, she turned to the statesman, retired now from political life, to express the hope that he would represent Israel at General de Gaulle's funeral.

Following the parliamentary elections of November 1965, Mrs Meïr resigned from the government. This allowed her to be named secretary-general of Mapai. Shortly before the Six-Day War, her opposition to Rafi led her to voice her disapproval at responsibility for the country's defence having been handed to Moshe Dayan.

By contrast, she was favourable to a rapprochement with Yigal Allon's Ahdut HaAvoda. Mapai's combination with it and Rafi led to the founding of the Labour Party in early 1968. Named the new party's secretary-general, Meïr then resigned within a matter of months. She was seventy years old, facing health problems and considering withdrawal from political life, when Eshkol's death persuaded her to reconsider. Previous opinion polls, which had given her at the most a 2% chance of assuming the premiership, could be discounted. The most significant part of an already full life was yet to come; its strangest day being that on which Israel's 'Grandmother' and President Sadat, in front of the bowled-over Jerusalem crowd, exchanged good-humoured pleasanteries with one another, as though they were long-lost friends.

Golda Meïr was born in Kiev (Ukraine) on 3 May 1898. She died on 8 December 1978 in Jerusalem.

Yasser Arafat

Mastermind of the Palestinian Cause

The dream the head of the PLO devoted forty years of his life to – seeing his national flag fly over Jerusalem – was not to be. Days before he died, the writer saluted the tenacity with which he had brought about recognition by the international community of the Palestinian people.

(2004)

Yasser Arafat would have liked to be remembered as the leader who succeeded in bringing peace and independence to his people. History, however, has turned out differently. Pronounced clinically dead on 4 November 2004, his spirit was finally worn down by time and the realisation that, after so many years, he was not going to reach the promised land.

And yet eleven years before, like the majority of Palestinians, he was convinced that this dream was now almost within grasp. They predicted six years – a drop in the ocean – of negotiations with Israel to clarify all the terms. This period has elapsed; their hope has worn thin. 13 September 1993 has apparently receded to a point in pre-history. That was the day when a very smiling

Yasser Arafat shook hands on the White House lawn with one of his greatest enemies, the Israeli prime minister, Yitzhak Rabin, in front of an invited audience of the world's leading figures and millions of television viewers.

In principle, the signing of the Oslo Accords placed one of the world's longest-running conflicts on track towards a resolution. This was the general belief, that Yasser Arafat shared. It was his tryst with destiny, the accomplishment of a long struggle and the first clear sign that the virtual Palestinian state, which had been proclaimed in Algiers on 15 November 1988 to an ecstatic Parliament-in-exile, would actually be achieved. (…)

Rooted out of the Lebanon, for six years the Palestinian Liberation Organisation (PLO) had continued its exile in Tunisia. In the eyes of Israel, the United States and a host of other countries it remained a terrorist group. Israel's liquidation of its leadership continued. (…) The Palestinians fell out amongst themselves. The support they received from Arab 'brothers' was neither unanimous nor unconditional. And yet Yasser Arafat remained steadfast, as he had been for forty years, in the cause, the establishment of a Palestinian state.

He was inspired, exclusively, by the justice of this cause and the people he represented. Those he antagonised did not really matter, while he was adept at drawing practical benefit from sympathisers. Allies and adversaries were both manipulated: some were flattered, others disdained. By turns, he could be familiar or distant, modest or arrogant, a generous benefactor or unflinching repudiator. However humble it might be, no support was ever overlooked; so the future should not be prejudiced, no bridge was ever burnt. Diplomacy and military action were used alternately or in combination.

Physically courageous, he would not abandon his supporters. Luxuries could be dispensed with but he valued honours, especially when bestowed by a foreign leader, as a form of recognition and support for the struggle against an enemy with the advantage of powerful sympathisers across the world.

It was not uncommon for members of his entourage to line their pockets, especially after the Palestinian Authority was set up in 1994. He did not deprecate it but he remained a man of simple tastes, for whom money had a restricted purpose as the ligament of war, and fund out of which to pay his followers and associates. The keys to the organisation's almost overfull treasury swung from his chain, finance being the main way in which the Arab world, particularly its oil-rich monarchies, was able to express its solidarity.

Operating within a thicket of resistance movements that were not always answerable to regimes favouring the PLO, Arafat had little alternative than to be a subtle manoeuvrer. He was also an autocrat, reserving the right to order detail, as much as strategy. To the regret of those obliged to keep up with him, this workaholic only needed a few hours' sleep per day. Without warning, or consideration for his comfort, he would be on the move, apparently relishing once more a near-homeless existence. Because his enemy was strong, he realised that he must be, not unlike an animal, on the alert for those who wished him dead. Luck played a part too: how many times did it seem as if his *baraka* had miraculously protected him from death and allowed him to carry on? For example in 1982, when the west Beirut building he had just walked out of was reduced to rubble by an Israeli bomb? Or, ten years later, when his plane crashed in the Libyan desert and he received nothing more than a few bruises?

Arafat's determination verged on obduracy. He would not concede either to himself that he might be wrong or, publicly, that he was beaten. Considering himself vested with a duty to his people that he must fulfil, his frequent threats of resignation were nothing more than a controlling technique.

In October 1990, after a hard struggle, and assured of the Occupied Territories' support, he eventually obtained the US' agreement in the Madrid Peace Process, that the PLO should be Israel's counterpart in talks. Another big effort was required from him to gain last-minute acceptance that it should be formally acknowledged as an Oslo Accords signatory.

The task Yasser Arafat had set himself was necessarily difficult. Then there were the added challenges of maintaining the resistance movements' unity, and also a sense of national identity amongst a people scattered around various host countries as well as the Occupied Territories.

A bloody petition

Following the creation of the Israeli state in 1948, Yasser Arafat took up political activity in Egypt. He had been born there on 4 August 1929, although some biographers accept the possibility, as he claimed, that Jerusalem was his birthplace. His father, originally from Gaza, had lived in Cairo since 1927: he may have recorded the boy's birth there so that he would receive free schooling; or his mother, who came from Jerusalem, may have chosen to spend her confinement at her parents', only registering the birth when she returned to Egypt and her husband. Mohammad Abdel Raouf Arafat Al-Koudwa Al-Husseini – soon known as Yasser (or 'easygoing') – Arafat was the sixth of seven rapidly appearing children. They all lived together until their mother died in 1933. His brother, Fathi, who would later become president of the Palestinian Red Cross, and he then went to live in Jerusalem with a maternal uncle, Salim Abou Saoud. The return to Cairo came four years later, when his father had remarried. This was where he received his education; subsequently he retained an Egyptian accent: quite unusual for a Palestinian.

His interest in politics was first aroused by the Muslim Brotherhood, champion at that time of Palestinian liberation. This liaison – he claimed to have only ever been a sympathiser – would permit Arafat, on the one hand, an acquaintance with Gamal Abdel Nasser's prison system and, on the other, to benefit from the grants that Saudi Arabia extended to Fatah, instead of the PLO, in the anti-Israel struggle.

In 1952, Arafat and the Gaza-born Salah Khalaf (Abou Iyad) took control of the Union of Palestinian Students. He presented a petition to General Neguib, Egypt's strongman. It consisted of the words: 'Do not forget Palestine', written in blood. But the 'Young Officers" was a regime only recently arrived in power and had other priorities. In 1957 Arafat left for Kuwait. A qualified engineer, he worked for the Public Works Department before setting up his own company which, if he is to be believed, made him, in quick time, a millionaire. He became friends with Abou Jihad who, in contrast to his own flamboyant and public style, preferred to work discreetly behind the scenes; he was to be his closest ally until 1988, when he was killed by an Israeli commando. The two opposites played their respective, indispensable roles in the national liberation movement. With a handful of other Palestinian exiles, that included Abou Iyad, they set in place the rudiments of a small military organisation: in October 1959 the clandestine Fatah was born.

Fatah means 'conquest'; it is the palindrome of Hataf (death), which is the acronym for Harakat al tahrir al watani al filistini (The Palestinian National Movement of Liberation). As he explained to his biographers, Janet and John Wallach, the movement's name is one that Arafat derived from the Koran, where it signifies 'the opening of the gates of paradise'. As for Abou Ammar, the *nom de guerre* that he adopted at this time – it refers to Ammar Ben Yasser, companion of the Prophet Muhammad. (...)

Emboldened by events in Algeria, where revolution had paved the way for independence, Yasser Arafat, renouncing a lucrative activity and style of life, was frequently absent from his engineering company, in order to visit the revolutionary cells that now existed in Egypt and Syria, Algeria and Jordan. Fatah's first official recognition came in 1963, when a bureau run by Abou Jihad was allowed to open in Algeria. The next year it set up a training camp close to Algiers. Recognition by Algeria opened other doors, notably to Mao's China, which Arafat visited in 1964.

Israel's decision that January to divert Lake Tiberias, so as to irrigate the Negev desert, led to an Arab summit in Cairo. President Nasser suggested the creation of an official Palestinian organisation to fight the Jewish state. It would consist of two arms, the political Palestinian Liberation Organisation and the military Palestinian Liberation Army, to which a number of Arab armies would lend expertise and leadership. Ahmad Choukeiri was chosen as the PLO's leader. Within three months it had adopted a charter calling for the State of Israel to be destroyed.

Extending the olive branch

So as to dispel the notion of its subservience to Egypt, Arafat's small Fatah group wanted to come out of the shadows and demonstrate its independence in a first military action against Israel. When the device left by its commando unit at a hydraulic plant did not explode and was defused by the Israelis, Fatah nevertheless produced its 'Communiqué No.1' to draw attention to the operation. Arafat had it circulated to Beirut's newspapers. The Israelis openly laughed at such amateurism. Amusement turned to anger after the Palestinians launched twenty-eight further commando operations towards the end of 1965.

It would take four years for Yasser Arafat to gain control of the PLO, which had been created not only without him but as a deliberate counterweight to his activity. These four years saw Fatah's guerilla warfare become both more effective and dramatic, to the point that the Arab countries from which the commandos' attacks were launched began to express reservations. The group's ranks had grown considerably, particularly after the Six-Day War of June 1967 and the loss of Gaza and the West Bank.

The disagreement with, and then loss of, Jordan as its principal base (1970-71) marked a dark period for the PLO, that lasted until the 1974 Arab summit, held in Casablanca, recognised it as sole representative of the Palestinian people. A type of consecration for Yasser Arafat, reinforced within a few months when, for the first time, he spoke to the United Nations' General Assembly. Once the PLO modified its Charter, so that now, instead of all the lands it staked a claim to, it would accept the establishment of a Palestinian state within agreed boundaries, Arafat felt able to present himself as a man of peace. But his holding out the olive branch was met with derision by the Israelis.

The following decade could hardly have turned out worse for him: the PLO's eviction from Beirut in 1982 was compounded in the tragedy of the Sabra and Chatila Palestinian refugee camp massacres. The next year, following a fratricidal struggle with other Palestinian and Syrian groupings, came a second expulsion, from Tripoli, the Libyan capital. Its exile now led to Tunisia. While the *Fedayeen* contested Israel throughout the Middle East – in Algeria and Yemen, Sudan and Iraq and Tunisia itself – the PLO could only look on. This was also the time when the repression of the Palestinian populations of Gaza and the West Bank intensified, to the point that it triggered an indigenous fightback. The children of the *Intifada* shouted out the PLO name and looked up to Yasser Arafat. They provided him with a first ray of light.

The revolt justified Arafat's 1988 proclamation of a virtual Palestinian state, based upon the UN Security Council resolutions 242 and 338, that, until now, had been rejected. These implicitly recognised Israel's right to exist. Arafat made numerous disavowals of terrorism, which were not yet strong enough for the US. Meanwhile, a dialogue had begun along hidden channels, with Sweden as intermediary. It was at a press conference, following an extraordinary meeting of the UN's General Assembly, that Yasser Arafat's firmer denunciation of terrorism persuaded Washington to finally say 'Yes' to direct talks with the PLO. They began, before long, in Tunis. Then, in May 1989, François Mitterrand's Paris guest delivered a prepared French text which implied that the clauses in the PLO's charter calling for Israel's destruction were now obsolete. The speech produced its desired effect, though Arafat knew that the PLO's legislative body, the Palestinian National Council, could alone make amendments to this document.

There was little time for him to enjoy these early, statesmanlike, successes before Saddam Hussein invaded and annexed Kuwait the following year. Arafat sounded out Palestinian opinion, generally favourable to the Iraqi leader. He encouraged a peaceful solution and did not condemn the action. The consequences for Arafat and the PLO were entirely negative. The Arab countries that had been his principal benefactors cut off all funding, while the Palestinian population of the Gulf States were expelled in their hundreds of thousands. The United States turned away. In effective quarantine when the First Gulf War ended with Kuwait's liberation, Arafat and his followers were barred from taking a part in talks aimed at a solution to the Israeli-Arab conflict. The only Palestinians admitted were representatives from the Occupied Territories.

It was they who provided a way out of the impasse. But it was the Chairman who directly handed them their instructions.

Yasser Arafat was born in Cairo (Egypt) on 4 August 1929. He was the first president of the Palestinian Authority, and in 1994 shared the Nobel Peace Prize with Shimon Peres and Yitzhak Rabin. On 29 October 2004 he was taken to Percy military hospital at Clamart (Hauts-de-Seine), where he died on 11 November. His funeral took place in Cairo the next day. He was buried in the Ramallah HQ compound, on the West Bank.

Juan Antonio Samaranch

Olympian Ambassador

For twenty-one years the Spaniard Juan Antonio Samaranch was president of the International Olympic Committee. During this time he succeeded in investing the role with a proper diplomatic significance. A potentate, part-pope, part-godfather of sport? Whilst he may have been all of that, the writer also accepts that this intriguing figure combined instinct with a rare persuasive gift, and ingenuity, too.

(2010)

Following a novel-like life, whose plot ran via plenty of twists and turns, and that was marked by ineradicable traits as well as temporary setbacks, Juan Antonio Samaranch, for twenty-one years the president of the International Olympic Committee, has died at the age of eighty-nine in his native city, Barcelona, this 21 April. He was a bourgeois of the city to his roots. Catalonia, comparatively, meant little to him. From this cosmopolitan vantage point he nursed his fascination for Catholic Madrid, and gave a free rein to the disdain he felt for the rest of his countrymen, whom he considered to be backward peasants.

On the one hand he was an extremely proud, ambitious man, a political animal and dangerous charmer; on the other, he was always a steadfast friend, irrespective of how dubious some of the circles he occupied might have been. The most Machiavellian of all Spaniards? The journalist Andres Marca Varela, who was an intimate of long-standing, described him as 'not necessarily a brilliant, more a deep intellect. Ponderous, but frighteningly resourceful'.

Samaranch's most serviceable maxim was: 'The best way to win a battle is not to fight it.' He had a gift, remarked the hero of Annapurna and de Gaulle's former minister of sports, Maurice Herzog, for 'strangling all opposition. His strength lay in the power with which he clasped his enemies to his breast. They would be paralysed, without the need to be snuffed out'. Within the sporting world he was known as 'Mr That Suits Me'.

His life's second act, dating from 1980, when he was elected to the IOC leadership, was performed with a bevy of ever-present advisers. As he intended, they competed with one another before he, unflinchingly, made the big decisions. When he retired, in 2001, these acolytes organised the type of send-off that Rome granted her victorious emperors. Thanks to him they were the new kings of sport.

A lucky man, who had the ability to capitalise on his opportunities. It should not come as a surprise that he made a fetish of the date 17 July. This was the date on which, in 1920, he was born into a very comfortably-off Barcelona family. On 17 July 1973 he was named president of the Regional Council, that presided over the province's affairs during Catalonia's phony autonomy within the Franco regime. Four years later to the day he became ambassador to Moscow. His presidency of the IOC, which was to last exactly twenty-one years, began on a 17 July.

17 July 1936 was also significant in the life of Juan Antonio Samaranch: the civil war was announced by Generals Sanjurjo and Franco, leading to the young Republic's defeat in 1939.

At the time Samaranch became its president, the IOC was scarcely more than a private members' club for a strictly limited number of European aristocracy. Halfway through his command, it had been transformed into a political body and the games invested with a new influence, twinned to funding that would not have been imagined before. Such success permitted the all-out Francoist, as he had been, a second bite of the cherry in his homeland. Already recipient of Francoism's highest sporting award, in 1990 he was honoured with democratic Spain's equivalent. In 1991 Juan Carlos elevated him to the title Marquis of Samaranch. These two distinctions fell either side of his becoming president of 'la Caixa', the country's No.1 building society.

One of Franco's blue-shirts

Juan Antonio Samaranch was no doubt better suited to the slalom's balancing act than to a more direct type of race. On becoming head of the IOC, he had much to do in order to gloss over the full extent of his support for the Franco regime. In 1972, three years before the *Caudillo*'s death, he stated, 'I am 100% Francoist'. But his first authorised biography would grant two paragraphs only to the twenty-five years in which he had diligently served his leader. Already with a foothold in the sporting hierarchy, the 1950s saw him join La Brigada del Amanecer (Dawn Brigade) which grouped together Barcelona's leading families, now profiting from the city's development.

From 1955 he was a member of the Falange, Francoism's fascist wing. Minister of sports in 1961, the following year he took control of the Spanish Olympic Committee. Membership of the IOC came in 1966. His devotion to the regime was highlighted in a photo his detractors were to make much use of, kneeling in front of Franco to swear a solemn oath. It was thanks to Francoism, he addressed those representing the country at the 1968 Olympics, that 'we Spanish are once more a virile race'.

Instead of the high office that he imagined he would attain, came the regime's final phase. Out of step with the times, he occasionally blundered. In 1974 the anarchist – and Catalan – Salvador Puig Antich was condemned to death. A fair number of the province's leading figures called on the government to show clemency. But, on 3 March, Puig Antich was nevertheless garotted. Juan Antonio Samaranch did not speak up.

He lent his support to the post-Franco claim of Don Juan de Borbón rather than his son, Juan Carlos, designated successor of the *Caudillo* himself. When the moment came he set up a new Francoist party in the province. Concordia Catalana was to last for three weeks: one hundred thousand protesters took to the streets in April 1977 chanting, 'Samaranch, *fot el camp*!' ('Samaranch, go!')

'He was finally prompted to unbutton his blue shirt and put on a fresh, neutral-coloured, replacement', as the Catalan human rights lawyer, Josep Benet would later remark. With Adolfo Suárez, the prime minister, he arranged to be appointed ambassador to Moscow. Given his long history of anti-communism this might appear a strange choice. But both Moscow's hosting of the next Olympics and his own good relations within the Eastern Bloc, that owed much to Adidas' boss, his friend Horst Dassler, favoured this step towards the IOC. With their support, Samaranch would campaign to take over over from the lacklustre Irishman, Lord Michael Killanin, as the committee's president. In 1980 he was duly elected to the post.

There were four elements to the construction of his IOC: solid, independent financial foundations; setting up a proper administration, answerable to himself; the support of leading politicians, financiers and industrialists; his own presentation on the world stage.

Twenty-five years later it is hard to find fault with the balance sheet: the committee's budget is twenty times that of 1980 and revenue from both sponsorship and broadcasting rights deals has risen exponentially. Pre-Samaranch, the 1976 Montreal games came to TV companies at a price of thirty-four million dollars; the figure agreed for the 2008 Beijing games was 1.7 billion. To be one of the 1988 Olympics' 'exclusive sponsors' cost ten million dollars; today's price is sevenfold.

The 'Coca-Cola Games'

An inevitable outcome of this commercialising trend came in 1988 when Juan Antonio Samaranch deleted the word 'amateur' from the Olympic Games' charter. The means now available to the IOC also began to provide a (more than) reasonable living for its members, whose number had grown from seventy-seven in 1980 to one hundred and thirty in 2001 and included ex-ministers, industrialist magnates and certain 'honorary members', such as Henry Kissinger and Giovanni Agnelli.

The crowning achievement that, during his reign, Samaranch insisted upon for the committee was that it should exercise diplomatic clout. Shuttling from one capital to another, the Olympics ambassador was able to turn the Games' consecutive boycotts (of Moscow 1980 by the US and other countries, and of Los Angeles 1984 by the Soviet Bloc) to the committee's advantage, as a potentially useful conduit for harmonious international relations. In this regard, the two accomplishments he was proudest of were directing the two Koreas to and at the negotiating table, in preparation for the 1988 Olympics then, four years later, instigating the UN's unanimous vote for an 'Olympics truce' that would allow athletes from the former Yugoslavian Republics to compete at Barcelona.

A consequence of his and the IOC's diplomatic standing was that, with one notable exception, it became arbiter of which city would host future Games. The political aspect of 'Seoul' was clear. 'Barcelona' was intended to set the seal on both the country's and Samaranch's transition from Francoism to democracy. Atlanta 1996, the 'Coca-Cola Games', symbolised the Games' progressive commercialisation.

Beijing, it was thought, would host the Games' 2000 edition. Instead, by voting for Sydney, a *camarilla* of the committee's loose cannon delivered a rare defeat to Juan Antonio Samaranch, who nevertheless ensured that the torch would be handed on to the Chinese capital in 2008.

Welcomed as a quasi-head of state wherever he travelled, the mid-'90s marked Samaranch's apotheosis. The backlash of his final mandate though was not long in coming and suggested that he had perhaps, at the age of seventy-eight, held the post long enough. In 1998, the Salt Lake City scandal erupted. As part of its effort to secure the 2002 winter Games, the American city had bribed IOC members to the tune of one million dollars. 'Time to go, M Samaranch,' led *Le Monde* on 26 January 1999. His reputation tainted, 'la Caixa' withdrew its chairmanship from him. An outraged US Senate summoned him to testify before its Commerce Committee. The senators too stressed to him that it was time to depart.

He stood his ground, however, and now undertook the reform

of the IOC so as to make it more accountable.

Ten members were fired. The scandal subsided. In Moscow, on the final day of his presidency, the Marquis of Samaranch was able to propose the election of his son, Juan Antonio Jr to the IOC. His American adversary, Senator John McCain regarded it as one 'final, nepotistic gasp'.

His residual influence, as honorary president of the IOC, appeared to be on the wane in Copenhagen on 2 October 2009. Speaking in this capacity, he confided to its members: 'You know that I am eighty-nine years old and nearing my end. Permit me to ask that you should consider the honour we would feel [Samaranch was speaking on behalf of Spain and Madrid, as a contending city] in hosting the 2016 Games.' The intervention, by one who had survived several attempts to get him to resign, was in vain. The Games were conferred on Rio de Janeiro.

A potentate, part-pope, part-godfather of sport? Undoubtedly, but there was much more to Samaranch than that: his progress from unalloyed Francoism to a proposal, latterly, of peaceful co-existence; his development from the bourgeois who found the whole idea of aristocracy so appealing, to the moment he purged the IOC of its class influence; his embrace of Africans, Asians and women within the Olympic institutions, having once been a confirmed believer in the West's continuing civilising mission.

He was what the Catalans call an *espavilat*, to suggest a blend of instinct, seductive charm and ruthless calculation, allied to resourcefulness. Juan Antonio Samaranch may be gone, but his paradox remains: in spite of grave personal failings, he stands as the Olympic ideal's greatest champion since Baron Pierre de Coubertin.

JUAN ANTONIO SAMARANCH

Juan Antonio Samaranch was born on 17 July 1920 in Barcelona, where he died on 21 April 2010. He was president of the International Olympic Committee (IOC) from 1980 – 2001.

Giovanni Agnelli

The Numero Uno Magnate

For fifty years the all-powerful president of Fiat symbolised the Italian dream. His reputation, that of a one-time playboy turned patriarch, exceeded that of most heads of state. Advocate, before the fact, of global liberalism, he led a life that resembled a self-penned fairy tale.

(2003)

In spring 1966 the automobile industry was taken unawares when Fiat made a pact with the devil, in the form of the USSR. The photo of Soviet foreign minister Andrei Gromyko shaking hands with Professor Valletta, *eminence grise* of the Italian group since the death of its founder, Senator Giovanni Agnelli, was to be seen everywhere in the weekly magazines. Standing one pace apart from these two figures was an elegant, still young man whose fit, good-looking appearance – bronzed, and greying at the temples – unavoidably suggested a patrician. As the caption made clear, this was the heir to, and current chairman of, the company. The choice of Giovanni Agnelli II, or 'Gianni' to distinguish him from his celebrated grandfather, was made with little fanfare and merited only a brief item in *Le*

Figaro. The general opinion was that it was probably a matter of form and nothing more; because, at forty-five, Gianni's renown still lay in the domain of a sophisticated, fast-living lifestyle. His interest in cars was apparently limited to driving them – too fast. Few doubted that the austere engineer, Gaudenzio Bono was to be Professor Valletta's ultimate successor, not this playboy...

Six months after his nomination, Agnelli made an impact with a one-off price reduction of 40% for drivers who found themselves without a car, following the recent floods. To the board of directors' bewilderment the following year he instituted what was destined to become the great journalistic event of his annual press conference, given on the fringe of the Turin show. Here he would discourse not just about Fiat's latest range but inflation and pollution, football and the state of the nation as well.

Recognition came within a matter of two years: for *Newsweek* Giovanni Agnelli was 'the man who had led his company to the top'; *Paris Match* photographed him at the wheel of his ninety-foot yacht, shirt discarded – but only because, at the same time, it was asking him for his perspective on the global automobile industry's future. For the next thirty years (and more) Fiat's, shortly followed by Italy's, image were to be conflated with that of Agnelli himself. At the same time that the memory of his illustrious grandfather faded, Professor Valletta's dominance was soon forgotten and the younger brother figure of Umberto almost overlooked, even though he too was now involved in the company's management. Gianni was affectionately recognised throughout Italy as *Il Avvocato* – 'The Lawyer' – on account of his (half-finished) law studies. He was also referred to as the *'Condottiere'*, the 'modern day Medici', 'the last of the Florentine princes', the 'king' or, more simply, the 'Great'

Agnelli. The paparazzi were never far away and adulation appeared his due. Imitated to the last detail, the world press treated each of his utterances as oracular.

A 1977 opinion poll quoted by *The Times* revealed that, whereas 99% of Italians knew who the pope was, 100% were familiar with Giovanni Agnelli, an obviously extraordinary degree of recognition. Which head of state, political or religious leader could lay claim to an equivalent level of fame? This can be assumed to be rarer still amongst industrialists. However hard one tries to discern one, there is no real comparison. If Henry Ford comes to mind, that is because mass production and the consumer economy both originated with him. Agnelli by contrast had simply managed – however successfully – a big company and its inherited wealth; Fiat may have been dominant in Italy but in a global context was not particularly spectacular. *Il Avvocato*'s claim to fame was not a pioneering breakthrough in the means of production but to have placed himself at the head in a domain that has since assumed strategical importance in business: communication. As the personification of enlightened capital, unafraid either to engage with the other principals or on the global stage, where he operated beyond the temporal power his position within Italy afforded him, he exercised a quasi-spiritual power over the western world's economy taken as a whole. His charisma helped Gianni become acknowledged as something of a worldwide advocate of liberalism. Amongst recognisable business leaders, he was the master.

It is unlikely that, at the very outset, this is what he had set out to be. However, earlier than anyone else in the field, he sensed the role that publicity was going to assume and set about innovating in it. Public relations at the time was limited to the corporate annual report. For Agnelli, however, a company's image had the potential to reflect back positively on its products and was therefore worth investing in. Fiat's publicity department was more than three hundred strong after 1970 and Gianni's interest in what the press said was keen. His legendary daily routine involved a thorough perusal of it by 7 am. He had close relations with Italy's principal newspaper editors and was apt to call them not much later in the morning to give his view of the news. He owned *La Stampa* and would later obtain a controlling interest in it, together with the peninsula's No.2 publication, the *Corriere della Sera*. There was also *La Repubblica*. 'My métier,' he explained, 'is one half management and one half communication.' With a natural enthusiasm for art and sport, he was the first, long before it became fashionable, to evolve corporate patronage. He was the owner of the football club his father had founded, which happened to be the most popular in the country: Turin's Juventus. In this and other historical cities the Fiat Foundation was involved in the restoration of palaces, churches and museums, such as Venice's Palazzo Grassi, whose spectacular exhibitions it curated.

Fiat's success gave *Il Avvocato* the assurance that he himself was its best advertisement. The jet-set habitué's aura – his natural elegance, international contacts and fluency in several foreign languages, and even his well earned reputation as a playboy – helped rather than hindered the business. Being secular, multicultural and democratic – in a word, modern – presented no danger to it at all. From the outset he put himself somewhere above the political mêlée and beyond the national frontier, unaffected by either; Italy was his base, but its internal politics bored him. 'Its particular culture is not for me.' His preferred field of action lay beyond any frontier. Leaving them behind in his private jet stream, as others would stops on the underground, his day might find him breakfasting in Rome, later dining in Paris, before returning in the evening to Turin, via St Moritz and an hour's skiing...

Gradually he realised the scale of power that his pre-eminence in the media sphere conferred. It allowed him to stand up for Fiat and the other companies he owned, privileging the very ideas that he wished to promote for their own sake. They were the basis of his repertoire as a member of the Trilateral Commission and countless other supranational think-tanks. The arguments he made for liberal economics and open markets, even if he recognised the need for social partnerships, were those of an advocate, before the fact, of both globalisation and a single European currency; he achieved instant recognition around the world as such.

'Giovanni Agnelli's power,' explained John Kenneth Galbraith, the economist, 'derived from an ability to think for himself that was without equal.' An intuitive and always curious approach led him to Yugoslavia, Poland, Bulgaria and Romania in advance of other business magnates. The groundbreaking visits he made to China, starting in 1975 before Mao had even died, provoked intense interest. In 1991 he ventured into virgin territory for a captain of industry when, succeeding Saul Bellow, he was invited to give the Romanes lecture at Oxford University. This consecration of *Homo Europeus* was shortly followed by an evening his old friends, Henry Kissinger, Lord Carrington, Rupert Murdoch and Oscar de la Renta organised, to which all the people that mattered came, for his seventieth birthday at New York's Metropolitan Museum.

His legendary charm

His drive and desire to inform himself, his position and links were beyond question. But there was something extra, indefinable, about him too. As one of his nephews admitted a while ago, 'I have often asked myself what it is that he has. Something likeable'.

What he had was class and panache or, as the Americans like to call it, glamour. 'Glamour' was his favourite word. Above it even there was his legendary charm, that brought together wit and social ease with beautiful manners and a touch of ennui. This capital charm was enough to seduce the most beautiful women, the media and, on the day that Leonid Brezhnev succumbed, communist leaders too.

'He has a similar kind of appeal to an actor,' said Fellini. 'Fortune picked him out as a winner; mount the man on a horse and he is a king.' Handsome and extraordinarily wealthy, an aristocrat and a benefactor, his celebrity reaches around the world. With Italy suffering an endemic crisis of authority he has stepped into the breach to fulfil the same role in the popular imagination as the Queen does in England. His life, closely followed by the press and the subject of innumerable best-selling biographies, is filled with palaces and princesses, feats of arms and drawing-room successes: a fairy tale.

The myth and reality of *Il Avvocato* are not so far apart. Giovanni Agnelli was born on 12 March 1921 at Villar Perosa, a small village not far from Turin where his great-grandfather, a well-established farmer, had bought a marquis' villa dating from the eighteenth-century. This family seat witnessed the first combustion engine his grandfather, a cavalry officer with a vehement taste for mechanics, put together. Not long after, in 1891, with some of his friends he set up at Turin 'Fabbrica Italiana Automobili Torino': Fiat. At the villa, Gianni grew up with his six brothers and sisters, dressed alternately in little Lord Fauntleroy lace and sailor suits, surrounded by German nannies and family retainers. The ambiance was easygoing and cosmopolitan. Edoardo, his father, had married a princess, Virginia Borbone del Monte, the daughter of an American mother and Italian aristocrat. Gianni learnt to ski at Sestrières, the resort his father had begun; he was also happy playing with his toy footballers painted in the colours of 'Juve', the family club which won five consecutive league titles between 1931 and '35.

The boy was intelligent, impulsive and, every now and again, insolent. While his grandfather, the senator took encouragement from this, Miss Parker, his English governess, was not so happy. 'Never forget that you are an Agnelli,' would come her reminder. Tragedy came to the family in 1935 when Edoardo met an horrific death: decapitation by a seaplane's propeller. His fifteen-year-old son succeeded him at the head of Juventus. Speaking of this precocious responsibility, he reflected how 'coming into a great inheritance is fortunate, but also a duty and a challenge that must be met'.

Henceforth Gianni would live every moment as though it were his last. 'He would never let up,' relates his sister Susanna, Italy's former foreign minister and the only sibling able to match the older brother, with his formidable popularity. Always doing something, impulsive and easily bored, he liked art, the sea and mountains. A landscape or a painting would move him but then he would rapidly move on. It was his mother who set the quick pace of life. At her Cap Martin villa Donna Virginia cultivated a natural talent for the fantastic and for hedonism. Her intimacy with the writer Malaparte was well known, to the old senator's evident displeasure.

'You have the necessary attributes to be a leader,' the patriarch announced to his descendant, 'if that is what you desire.' But it was still a lot too soon.

Casino tables, fast cars, pretty girls

Aged seventeen, Gianni was sent to the US to learn about the automobile industry. His visit was cut short and he returned to Turin when war broke out. Legal studies were brought to a premature end too, when the twenty-year-old man left for the Russian front as part of Mussolini's army. Subsequently he fought and was decorated in Tunisia, before joining the Legnano brigade of the Italian Liberation Corps in 1943, to fight alongside the American army. It was a front-line war for him. Recalling it much later (to *France-Soir* in April 1996) he would confess: 'It's a terrible thing to say but I enjoyed the war. If one is twenty years old and there is a war, that is where one wants to be – not 'grounded' with the women and priests. That's not on. One should never let oneself be sidelined in life. My inclination was always to join the action.'

The war left him wounded in the leg and, with the death of Donna Virginia, an orphan. This was a difficult period: the senator had arrived at a long-term accommodation with Mussolini and had managed to persuade the Germans not to dismantle the factory. At the same time, he was discreetly lending his support to the Partisans. Nevertheless, in 1945 the government obliged him to step aside for 'supporting fascism'. Rehabilitation only came after his death. Gianni, who was aggrieved by what he considered 'a serious injustice', became a member of the board of directors. The time had come for him to choose between Fiat or relative obscurity. Professor Valletta had assumed the running of the company, shortly after his grandfather died, asking: 'The chairman of Fiat will be me or you?'

'You,' he replied. The reason was that 'I did not feel ready'.

Confining himself to the management – from a distance – of a small subsidiary producing ball-bearings, *Il Avvocato* now set out on a dazzling career as an international playboy. The question was to be frequently asked whether his grandfather had counselled him to make the most of his youth. To begin with Agnelli left it unanswered; later he would deny the suggestion. With an estimated one million dollar annual allowance at his disposal, he blazed a trail between his Turin mansion and St Moritz chalet, his yacht and a luxury villa at Villefranche-sur-Mer, which had previously belonged to the king of Belgium.

Early to rise, his days were spent rather like an athlete's, but at night-time on the Riviera he burnt the other end of the candle with the likes of Errol Flynn, Porfiro Rubirosa, the Aga Khan and Prince Rainier of Monaco. It was a period of his life when he claimed to be only interested in 'gaming tables and racing cars and pretty girls'. He was rumoured to have had affairs with Anita Ekberg, Rita Hayworth, Danielle Darrieux and Pamela Harriman, who had previously been married to Randolph Churchill. The future Jackie Kennedy visited him at his villa. True or false? When pressed on the point he would reply, 'I may occasionally talk to ladies but never about them'.

A serious accident, occurring on the Monaco road at 5 am one early morning in 1952, interrupted *La Dolce Vita*. His female passenger was unhurt but one of Agnelli's legs was badly fractured, leaving him with a slight limp. Although it did not prevent him from continuing to ski, the leg supported with a leather brace, the accident has often been cited as a turning point in his life. The truth is simpler: he was thirty years old and wanted to settle down. In 1953 he married Marella Caracciola di Castagnetta. As well as being a Neapolitan princess she was also a fashion photographer and amongst the ten best-dressed women in the world. 'The Italian Swan,' Truman Capote named her. Their marriage, which would produce two children, featured on the cover of *Vogue.*

Little by little, Gianni became more involved with the management of the Fiat empire, still controlled by the iron hand of the ageing – now more than seventy-five years – Professor Valletta. In 1959 he assumed the chairmanship of IFI, a holding company his grandfather had created in order to guide and guard the family fortune. 'My grandfather created Fiat and my responsibility, which I have never doubted, is to develop it.'

This did not prevent the Italian Communist Party's mouthpiece, *L'Unità* from commenting: 'Anything is possible at Fiat at the moment - other, that is, than one of the Agnellis being boss of the company begun by the old autocrat, their grandfather.' In 1963, Gianni was nevertheless designated the next head of Fiat. Whilst Agnelli may have been ready, Professor Valletta temporised. 'Fiat was his life, so he was always putting off retirement.'

When, finally, Giovanni took up the post in 1966, little was expected of him. Judged to be too superficial and lacking sufficient patience, no one really 'got him'. They did not understand that, now he had reached forty-five years of age, *Il Avvocato* had fallen upon a new addiction: power, with its corollary of work. The excessive energy – or competitive *grinta* – hitherto channelled into the pursuit of pleasure found this new focus instead. That did not mean he was suddenly forsaking sport or the high life. The reporter handed a 1968 assignment to accompany him for a single day returned exhausted at the end of it. Ready at 7 am, Giovanni had gone by helicopter from Villar Perosa to Turin airport and from there in his private jet to Rome, where he attended a Montedison directors' meeting.[1] At 1.15 pm he made the twenty minute return journey to Turin for a lunchtime meeting with a Milanese banker. Following a quick, but obligatory, siesta he and his Ferrari were Milan-bound to meet a Soviet leader. Coming back the needle touched 200 km/h. At Villar Perosa he then chaired a meeting of the local council before regaining his Turin mansion.

It was not uncommon for him to punctuate his day with an hour of skiing, or to nip over to London, where he could buy a painting at his friend and adviser David Somerset, the Duke of Beaufort's gallery. His private collection was one of the world's finest and included works by Picasso, Canaletto, Delacroix, Klimt, Matisse, Bacon, Roy Lichtenstein and Andy Warhol.

There was a great deal for the new chairman to do. Because of the success of its '500', Fiat was now the No.2 European car constructor. But it had a much too centralised management, with fixed and increasingly out-of-date ideas; Professor Valletta alone knew each car's cost price. Giovanni threw open the windows. He broke the old guard's hold and delegated. Umberto, his younger brother by thirteen years, was called into action, so that Agnelli himself could concentrate on strategy, top-level contacts and the big negotiations. Fiat needed to grow, and quickly, because if Europe could then count forty car manufacturers, within ten years, he warned, only a handful would remain: he wanted to be amongst them.

In 1968 he reached an agreement with Citroën's owners, the Michelin family. It envisaged their two companies' merger. But the suggestion that Citroën, the maker of his very own DS, should fall under Italian control was not acceptable to General de Gaulle. He gave the order to 'find me a national solution!' Four years of tense negotiations thus came to nothing, as Peugeot instead took the role. Subsequent attempts to buy Saab or Volvo and to form a partnership with Renault would also prove fruitless. Limited to the Italian peninsula, Agnelli had to admit that his dream of a Great Federation, a European 'General Motors' had failed. This would remain the one regret of his long career. Later, somewhat ironically, it was General Motors which, in 2000, was called to the rescue of the Italian manufacturer.

A state within a state

Constrained by capitalism's national identification to remain close to the enterprise's geographical origins, Gianni looked for other solutions. Even before the first oil shock of 1973, he understood how the car industry was particularly vulnerable to economic cycles. 86% of the Agnelli fortune was then tied up in the automobile sector: the time had come to diversify. *Il Avvocato* sought the advice of *Il Marionettista*, or 'Puppet Master', Enrico Cuccia, the managing director of Mediobanca, who pulled the strings of many an Italian governing board. With the inevitability of gradualism, the next thirty years saw IFI, the family holding company, place its supervisors throughout the economy: the leisure industry (Club Med, Accor); the leading distribution networks (Rinascente, Continent); the cement sector; publishing; food and drink production (Saint-Louis, Danone, Château Margaux); insurance and banks, etc.

Events justified this strategy. As of 1972, the decade was to be one of social conflict; the following year, Fiat's empire, which the oil crisis had not spared, recorded its first loss. Giovanni hinted that he might step aside and was offered the ambassadorship in Washington: was this to be the end of his seven-year reign? No: as during the war, he would remain in the 'front line', to fight on. In 1974 he was chosen as head of Confindustria (Italian equivalent of the CBI). With Luciano Lama, the trade union leader, he signed an 'historic' social contract that improved workers' purchasing power. Whilst inflation was given a stimulus, Fiat, like other Italian companies

, was able to take advantage of successive devaluations, by conquering European export markets.

Bolstered once more, by this success, he was briefly tempted to play a political role. Both his friends and his sister Susanna, a (centrist) Republican Party senator urged him to lend his weight to a broad political front that aimed to confront, with its own lay values, the all-powerful Christian Democrats who, 'with 40% of the vote', as he put it, 'had an 80% hold on power'. In the end he decided not to take up the challenge; he was happy to continue as mayor of Villar Perosa... The power he already possessed at Fiat, which amounted to a state within a state, was greater than any elected figure might expect. Benito Craxi's former favourite, Claudio Martelli defined it more precisely, as a 'monarchy within the republic'. Regarding renown: was there anyone, the pope included, he need envy?

The 1970s' social conflict took its toll on Fiat. Heeding Enrico Cuccia's advice, Agnelli let his brother go and replaced him with Cesare Romiti, a manager with very clear ideas who, within two years, was exercising the same role for him as Professor Valletta had for his grandfather. The two men were alike in their taste for risk, enthusiasm for football and deep commitment to the business. Romiti was something more than a right-hand man: rather like a major-domo, he could be counted on to deal with all the dirty work, such as the 1976 negotiations with Gaddafi for Libya to acquire a stake in the company, an outcome met with stupefaction throughout Italy, and displeasure on the part of the United States. In 1979 his task was to face down the unions and fire sixty-one workers, suspected of having terrorist links.

Social issues seemed by 1980 to be on the verge of carrying the company away. That year alone nine million man hours were lost to strikes. In the previous five years four board members had been killed and twenty-seven wounded by terrorists; middle management was menaced too and found it safer working from their suburban villas. The Red Brigades stalked Giovanni, who was unable to stay in the same place for more than two hours without risking serious danger. Across from the Quirinal Palace, the security that guarded him in his opulent apartment, brimming with works of art, exceeded that of a head of state.[2]

Nevertheless, he was not going to be harassed out of Italy. The family were instructed not to pay a ransom in the event of his kidnap. Romiti was entrusted with full powers. In September, after the factory had been brought to a standstill by a thirty-five-day strike, forty thousand management and workers took to the streets to demand the 'right to work'. The 'March of the Forty Thousand' was to prove a turning point. With immediate effect, social agitation was brought to heel; Fiat was saved. As profits soared, by 1986 Giovanni bought out the Libyan holding. 'It had caused one or two problems, of an almost aesthetic kind,' he explained. The following year he modified the company's identity to that of a limited partnership, with the purpose of securing family members' shares in the company, and to ensure that, with the coming generation, the expanded clan should still remain united.

Il Avvocato would soon be seventy. The well-known laureate's profile was slightly etched with age and, while his engaging look and smile had lost none of their charm, his features' fine definition had, little by little, thickened out. Following cardiac surgery he fell at his Roman home and broke his leg; this made headline news. Without enthusiasm, he was turning his thoughts to the succession. Edoardo, the direct descendant, had been discounted. The relationship of a son deeply involved in philosophy and eastern religions and his father had never been easy. When, in 1990, he had been questioned by Kenyan police for possession of drugs, Giovannini, his cousin was dispatched to sort the situation out. The son of Umberto was in fact the image of Edoardo's father at the same age: good-looking, athletic and elegant, endowed with ceaseless funds of energy. As time went by, it was clear that he was the favourite. Considering a staged succession the way to avoid potential friction, Agnelli envisaged transferring the presidency to Umberto, who would then make way, at an appropriate future date, in favour of his son.

Then the Gulf War intervened, leaving Europe in recession and the car industry confronting a further crisis. Once more, in 1992, Fiat was cutting costs and laying workers off. Its survival would call for massive reinvestment – double or quits. Seeing that it was not an advisable moment to retire, and under pressure from his taskmaster at Mediobanca, Enrico Cuccia, Giovanni delayed his departure. His brother was sidelined for a second time, as Cesare Romiti's position centre stage was reiterated. Robots arrived in the factories, taking the place of twenty-four thousand workers who had been shed.

By 1996 the enterprise was in provisional good health. With his job accomplished, Giovanni could finally retire, at the age of seventy-five. He was named 'Senator for Life' by the president of the Republic, while remaining as the group's honorary chairman. Romiti succeeded him as managing director, for the time it would take the next generation of Agnellis to emerge. The deserved retirement was covered by the world's press: Gianni, weakened after a second heart operation, found himself on the front pages once more.

Maturing into a business patriarch he had lost none of his playboy aura. Now the pace of life diminished a little more, the patrician fulfilling his role, not without dilettantish charm, as a cultivated and experienced elder. His friends were drawn from amongst the world's greatest names. He was an attentive grandfather, as pictures of him with his wife and the younger ones at the villa with its roses illustrated. Other images showed him by himself, calm and vaguely disinterested. In his interviews he spoke less about the life he was now leading, than of 'the crisis of the ruling classes', or of big business being under attack. While his personal prestige was unaffected, the Fiat company was not left untouched by 1993's operation 'Clean Hands'. Giovanni Agnelli made a public statement, expressing regret that his 'negligence' had contributed to the apparent 'corruption' of one of the group's subsidiaries. He wondered aloud, 'where does corruption end and racketeering begin? The dividing line between them is a narrow one...'

Realising the Italian dream

His retirement was, in fact, only partial. Whilst handing over the reins at Fiat itself, he maintained a firm control of the Agnelli limited partnership's strategy and, even more, the affairs of IFI which, over the years, had spread in a byzantine and international fashion. He had distanced himself but, in his own words, he was still 'in contact'. Cesare Romiti's attempt to stay on, when he reached retirement age in 1998, was not acceptable to *Il Avvocato*, who then imposed his own choice, recruited from General Electric. The decision, which followed the tragic deaths of Giovannini, his favourite nephew, and Edoardo, his son, to make a Fiat director of John Elkann, one of the family's next generation, was his.[3] So too was the conceit of marrying Fiat to General Motors. The dowry offered to the American firm was 20% of the Italian party's capital (with an option, as of 2004, on the remainder). In exchange, the Agnelli family became the American multinational's second largest shareholder. In July 2001 the eighty-year-old provided his countrymen with a further surprise when, in alliance with EDF, he launched a hostile bid for Montedison.

2002 brought another disappointing set of results, which saw Fiat drop to seventh position in the European car manufacturers' rankings. The family was forced to contemplate an impending sale. With General Motors poised, Italy shuddered. It was the return of the clan chieftain, still ill, from New York, where he had been receiving treatment, that signalled a fightback: he was not going to be funeral director of the empire his grandfather had founded. Even if it meant selling 34% of Ferrari, the Turin firm would have to be restructured. A trusted ally of the family was handed the delicate task of maintaining Fiat in a new balancing act between trade unions, banks and the state. But the question as to whether Fiat could outlast its legendary owner was now being openly posed.

What was beyond doubt was that forty years of struggle, patience and cunning had paid off for Giovanni Agnelli. Fiat had survived and, in spite of the alliances it had to form in order to do so, the family retained its controlling interest. His personal fortune was an estimated three billion euros. The ideological balance sheet looked more sanguine still: (his) liberal theories' triumph had left communism on the losing side; economic globalisation was now a fact, and European union had progressed, with Italy sharing its common currency. He might no longer be active, in the 'front line' as he had been, in one form or another, throughout his life, but this did not really matter: he had already done it all, earning a special and enduring place in Italians' hearts as *The* Boss, a type of *pater familias* personifying the best that the Italian dream had to offer. Speaking to *L'Express* in 1992 he shared his view that 'I have experienced all the phases of Italy's recent history: the war, the reconstruction which followed, that led to the economic miracle and *La Dolce Vita*. Terrorism too. And, because of all that experience, I have ended up as something of a reference point'.

Giovanni Agnelli was born in Turin (Italy) on 12 March 1921, where he died on 24 January 2003. On 21 April 2010 his thirty-four-year-old grandson, John Elkann succeeded to the Fiat chairmanship, which Luca Cordero di Montezemolo had held since the death of Il Avvocato.

Winston Churchill

The Unique Sir Winston

He is remembered as Britain's wartime prime minister. But Winston Churchill was also orator, writer and visionary. The author recalls this 'extraordinary character', who said of himself, 'we are all worms, but I do believe that I am a glow-worm'.

(1985)

'Today I am twenty-five years old. It is terrible to think how little time remains' – following a career in which he had been chancellor of the exchequer, as well as leader of the House of Commons, Lord Randolph Churchill's death, caused by venereal disease, had marked his son deeply: he imagined that he, too, would die young. Then, gradually, as he grew older, he realised that the constitution he had inherited was the robust American one of his mother, Jennie Jerome and her ancestors. His fate was to continue, as the physically diminished victim of several strokes, until he was ninety.

Who could fail to remember the sight of him as he had to be slowly eased down the boarding stairs of the airplane that had brought him to Bermuda, mechanically giving a 'V' for victory sign to the Royal Welsh Fusiliers' goat-mascot? Or, following his retirement as prime minister, the poignant moment when the Chamber's double doors were opened to allow the octogenarian 'Commons man', whose verve and wit had so often animated the House, to take up his place between two other backbenchers – a supporting role he resumed quite happily, especially for Prime Minister's Questions?

Four years before his death he was still sufficiently alert to follow debates. The suggestion, 'Speak to him loudly, he's very deaf,' made by one member to another, when Sir Winston failed to offer a conversational response, prompted the familiar voice to murmur, 'Yes, and they reckon he's gaga too'. He continued to smile at this, but it was as if he was marooned in his own world, dreaming perhaps of long ago...

Because he thought he would not have long to live, young Winston – left to his own devices by his parents and much closer emotionally to his nanny, Mrs Everest, a photo of whom he kept in his study at Chartwell for the rest of his life – was in a hurry to achieve great feats, in emulation of his famous eighteenth-century ancestor, the first Duke of Marlborough.

Just as both his father and the hero of Blenheim had been prone to mood swings, Winston suffered bouts of depression, melancholy moments, and even a pair of phobias: he did not like to sleep by a balcony and was wary when on station platforms. But in spite of these encounters with 'black dog', as he referred to them, his determination to rise to any challenge, including that of being relatively short, was clear. He did not hesitate to engage with life to the full, to act with conviction and, resisting adversity, to carry out sublime feats. He had been neither a particularly happy nor easy child; at school, conscious of the distance at which his parents held him, he found the classes too rigid and was a less than brilliant pupil. Considering his outcast status he drew, like the soldiers on the Sambre-et-Meuse had, on 'glory for his sustenance'.[1] He was confident that an important destiny awaited him. 'We are all worms, but I do believe that I am a glow-worm,' he confided to Violet Bonham-Carter. Military manoeuvres that he executed with a thousand toy soldiers sustained his imagination. He read the classics. Poetry, and Shakespeare in particular, appealed to him. Much later, there was an occasion when Richard Burton was led to distraction by the PM, seated in the front row, joining in Hamlet's most anguished soliloquies. Churchill's journalistic and performing talents were developed at a young age, and he was to put both to good use.

'I am getting to like soldiering'

When his father steered him towards the army, he twice failed to get into Sandhurst (the British St-Cyr). Showing his determination that, as a descendant of Marlborough, he could not forsake a military career, he succeeded at the third attempt.

The younger Randolph, with his father's Sandhurst experience in mind, later wrote that, 'He had to battle throughout his life... Nothing came easily to him, not even the speech-making or writing, that he came to master... First he had to develop the habit of intense concentration, which would later serve both himself and his country'.

'I am increasingly getting to like the profession of soldier, but at the same time I am more than ever certain that it is not actually mine,' Winston expressed his reservations. He enjoyed the adventure and the danger, as well as participating in military operations. The first war he witnessed was Cuba's revolt against Spain. Here he developed a taste for first hand knowledge – and siestas. On detachment from his regiment, India was his next destination. He went as a war correspondent, to accompany the Bengal Lancers. Fighting against tribesmen by sword, he was lucky to avoid being killed, before returning to the colours in the Sudan where Kitchener, Sirdar of Egypt, was waging war against the Mahdi and his Dervish forces. At the Battle of Omdurman, Churchill killed at least a few of their number in the bloody charge's hand-to-hand fighting.

Having continued writing throughout his military career, and being equally adept with a pen as a lance, he now related the story of this historic charge in a big book, which criticised Kitchener for commanding the Mahdi's tomb to be desecrated.

His preference for journalism grew stronger and, at the age of twenty-five, he set off to cover the Boer War. This was not without risks: during the course of an engagement young Winston was taken prisoner. It was the one capitulation in his lifetime and Louis Botha, later prime minister of South Africa, happened to be his captor. An action-packed escape from Pretoria prison began when he hid in the WCs; although the Boers offered £25 for his recapture, dead or alive, he succeeded in making his way back to England. The prison flag later found its way into his possession. In spite of burning it, his recommendation was that the Boers, who had proved themselves 'a worthy and honourable enemy', should be treated with moderation and understanding.

A continual ascent

Churchill's political career began with the new century. He idolised the memory of the gifted Conservative politician his father had been, whose career had, nevertheless, been waylaid by a volatile nature and then, decisively, illness. Maybe the son wanted to redress the defeats inflicted on the father about whom, although they had not enjoyed intimacy, he had written an appreciative biography full of insight; or, alternatively, he may have hoped to transcend a presence that had haunted his early life. Whichever the case, politics presented itself as at least the equal of war for danger and intrigue. 'In war you can only be killed once,' he said, 'but in politics many times.'

His own career would, in time, be marked by a succession of such 'deaths', followed by revival. They resulted from his temperamental and social inability to fit into any of the traditional hierarchies represented by party politics: his personality was a little too colourful, strong and unpredictable. The aristocracy, cosmopolitan middle-, and working classes were all unable to claim his allegiance. In a word, he was the perfect example of an outsider.

It did not take long for the young Member for Oldham to draw attention to himself by stepping outside the limits imposed by party discipline, criticising both government policy towards the Boers, and Chamberlain's protectionism. When the *enfant terrible* rose to speak at a party meeting in May 1904 he provoked whistles from his colleagues and prime minister, who then walked out of the hall. Within days his break with the Conservatives was official: he was elected Liberal MP for Manchester. Lloyd George was his new ally.

The Welshman, who had risen from unspectacular origins, exercised a particular appeal for the patrician Churchill. He gave him an insight into an England that, until now, Churchill had not really known. This was Dickens' world, in which the victims of the industrial revolution lived in slum dwellings and in poverty. The scion of a great family placed himself in the vanguard of the contest over House of Lords reform. He described it as 'an institution that was completely out of touch with the spirit of the time and the direction society was moving in'. At the same time he was quick to state his opposition to socialism, which 'undermined wealth, business and the individual'.

His rapid ministerial progress followed a classic pattern: under-secretary of state for the colonies, then president of the Board of Trade. Next, as home secretary, he piloted penal reform, although Churchill was best remembered by the public for the role he assumed in the 'Siege of Sidney Street'. This was the insalubrious East End address where armed anarchists were hiding from the police and Scots Guards, and which he attended dressed in a top hat.

The secretary's ambitions went further than his current office. In 1911 the Agadir incident incited him to repeatedly speak out against the threat Germany now posed. The Committee of Imperial Defence was impressed, to the point that, in October, Asquith finally awarded him the coveted post: First Lord of the Admiralty.

He eagerly sent ageing admirals on their way; a flurry of reforms were set in motion. To those who complained: 'But secretary, you can't do that, it goes against two centuries of Naval tradition', the First Lord replied: 'And what are those traditions? Rum, sodomy and the lash!'

When the August 1914 ultimatum to Germany expired, not wanting to let even the first minute pass, he had a telegram, that was unauthorised by the government, transmitted to all mobilised ships: 'Begin hostilities against Germany immediately.'

The events of the following year obliged him to back down, when he was held responsible for the Dardanelles disaster and dismissed from the Admiralty, which he would not regain until 1940. 'One of the darkest periods in my life', he was to write. 'Like a sea-beast fished up from the depths, or a diver too suddenly hoisted, my veins threatened to burst upon the fall in pressure.'

A timely new enthusiasm appeared to soften the blow of his enforced retirement: 'And then it was that the Muse of Painting came to my rescue – out of charity and out of chivalry, because, after all, she had nothing to do with me.' He departed for the front, as his ancestor – the Malbrouk of the song – once had. 'When would he return?' sang his friends.

The return and answer came sooner than expected. Disregarding the Conservatives' protests, Lloyd George found room for him in the coalition government, as minister of munitions. In fact, Churchill would range well beyond this domain, to be a tribune for the anti-Bolshevik interventionist cause and to speak against defeatism on the Home Front. 'No peace until victory,' he exhorted a country that had wearied of the trenches' bloodletting. In 1919 he moved on to the War Office; his return to the Colonial Office came two years later. Now secretary, he worked out solutions both for Ireland and the Middle East which both, regrettably, had a short life expectancy.

A salutary period in the wilderness

A difficult period was marked by the 1922 election, the Liberal Party's effective death-knell. He lost his seat and, shortly after, had to undergo an appendix operation. As he put it: 'For the first time I found myself without an office, without a seat, without a party and without an appendix.' Two further electoral setbacks came in quick succession before he crossed back to the Conservative side. Baldwin appointed him as his chancellor, an office that he had some difficulty occupying. He would subsequently remark, 'Everyone said I was the worst chancellor of the exchequer that ever was, and now I am inclined to agree with them'.

Churchill's ten-year-long exile from politics began with Labour's return to power in 1929. As a writer and journalist it would be a productive period for him. At Chartwell he was able to read, maintain a production of journalistic pieces and write a nine-volume life of his ancestor, Marlborough. Visiting friends would be treated royally at his table. 'I am easily satisfied with the best,' he conceded. Good food and wine, not to mention whisky and soda, were in plentiful supply.

Clementine (or 'Clemmie') shared in his exile as, from the day of their marriage – when he and Lloyd George were discussing the subject, even in the vestry – she had shared Winston with this one, formidable rival: politics. The mutual affection of 'Pig' and 'Cat', as she and he nicknamed one another, was made clear in their daughter, Mary Soames' book. 'Your love for me is the greatest glory and recognition that has or will ever befall me,' he wrote her. During the 1930s Chartwell operated rather like a government-in-exile. From this base he started, even before Hitler arrived in power, to warn of Germany's re-emergence as a military threat. But Churchill's reputation as belligerent, rash, unpredictable and capricious had grown too strong; hardly anyone, his political family included, was listening.

Events bore him out. 'You were given the choice between war and dishonour. You chose dishonour and you will have war', he wrote the prime minister, when Chamberlain returned from Munich. A year later Hitler unleashed *blitzkrieg* on Poland and Churchill was recalled to the Admiralty.

'Blood, sweat and tears'

His destiny proved strong enough for Churchill's own Narvik

raid failure to precipitate Chamberlain's downfall. He was finally in command.

He 'mobilised', as President Kennedy described, 'the power of words and sent them into battle'. But a great effort was required of him in order that the handicap of a congenital speech defect (his difficulty in pronouncing 'S's), allied to a slight stammer, was not also an inconvenience. Like Demosthenes once had, Churchill practised assiduously, until he was finally able to master his delivery. He cultivated the art of the pause, learnt to emphasise vowels as he diminished consonants, in a vocabulary rich in striking expressions. These accumulated in a staccato style, mingled with quotes and poems that he knew by heart. 'I have nothing to offer but blood, toil, sweat and tears', was the key of his first speech. His strategy? 'To wage war'. The goal? 'Victory – victory at all costs, victory in spite of all terror, victory however long and hard the road may be; for without victory there is no survival,' In deed, as opposed to rhetoric, he gave a persistent and passionate, but occasionally blind lead, seen, for example, in the tragedy of Mers-el-Kébir.[2]

Twenty-four hours after Dunkirk, when the starkness of Britain's solitary stand was evident, Churchill's own emotion showed too. His secretary remembers how his voice suddenly gave way as he dictated his famous speech, 'We shall fight on the beaches, we shall fight on the landing grounds, we shall fight in the fields and in the streets, we shall fight in the hills'. His face was covered in tears. Gripping the back of a chair for support, he concluded, 'We shall never surrender', his voice triumphant.

Victory took precedence over all other considerations. Hitler having invaded the Soviet Union, the anti-communist crusader was paying due respect, within twenty-four hours, to the Russian troops 'standing on the threshold of their native land', set to struggle against the 'dull, drilled, docile, brutish masses of the Hun soldiery'. He made it clear: 'Any man or state who fights against Nazism will have our aid.' The biting eloquence with which he denounced Hitler throughout the course of the war sustained the morale of both his own and the conquered peoples of Europe, a well-known example being: 'This monstrous abortion of hatred and defeat, with his tattered lackey Mussolini at his tail.'

In advance of their 1941 meeting to draft the Atlantic Charter he assured Roosevelt that, if he would 'give us the tools ... we will finish the job'. After Pearl Harbour he told the president by telephone, 'we are all in the same boat now'. 'That night,' he would later write, 'I went to bed and slept the sleep of the saved and thankful.'

With unflagging energy he travelled the world to hasten victory and plan for peace. One of the 'Big Three', he attended all the conferences: Moscow and Casablanca, Tehran, Quebec and Paris.

It was in the middle of the concluding conference at Potsdam that the 'Old Lion' was electorally ousted by Labour and Attlee, 'a modest man, who has much to be modest about'.

Once more he was out of office. This latest hiatus in a roller-coaster career would last until his 1951 return to Downing St. In the interim, his evocation, at Fulton, Missouri in March 1946, of an iron curtain drawn across the continent was itself a curtain raiser for the Cold War. Having returned to the old continent, at Zurich he recommended the novelty of European unification, though later he was careful to repeat that, if it came to a choice between the two, Great Britain would surely be pulled towards the open sea and, therefore, the United States.

Churchill believed, in spite of his long-term anti-communism, that he was still, aged seventy-nine, the best negotiator to sit down with Stalin and find a solution to the world's problems. A meeting of the four Great Powers was justified, he felt, by the West's strong position. The Geneva Summit would take place, but neither Stalin, following his death in 1953, nor Churchill, having passed the premiership on to Anthony Eden in 1955, were in attendance.

The final time Churchill sat in the House of Commons was on 27 July 1964. His fellow parliamentarians paid their respects; he did not say a word. The following month he was taken into hospital. When Eisenhower visited him, he just had the strength to hold out a trembling hand and place it in that of his brother-in-arms. According to witnesses, neither man spoke as they remained like this for several minutes.

On 9 January 1965 Sir Winston declined the customary cigar and whisky. His final words, spoken to his family, were: 'The journey was interesting and well worth the taking – once.' Then he fell asleep and went into a coma. He died on 24 January, the seventieth anniversary of his father's death, as he had predicted to his secretary.

Churchill was many things: a man of action and statesman, writer and journalist, an orator and a visionary; each of us retains a memory of some facet of this extraordinary and appealing character. For de Gaulle, he was 'the great champion of a great undertaking and the great artist of a great history'.

Winston Churchill was born on 30 November 1874 at Blenheim Palace (Woodstock, Oxfordshire), the ancestral seat of the Dukes of Marlborough. He died in London on 24 January 1965.

Notes

CHARLES DE GAULLE

1. (1878-1966) Prime minister of France from March 1940.

2. (1901-65) Real name Henri Petiot. A Catholic writer, his faith lapsed in the 1920s. He refound it amidst the secular extremism of the '30s. Daniel-Rops directed the collection 'Présences' for Plon and published de Gaulle's *La France et son armée* (*France and her Army*).

3. (1715-47) Luc de Clapiers, marquis de Vauvenargues was chiefly known for a collection of essays and aphorisms published in 1746 with the encouragement of his friend, Voltaire. A moralist writer, he is regarded as a modern stoic.

4. At the outbreak of World War II, General Henri Giraud (1879-1949) was a member of the Superior War Council. He disagreed with de Gaulle over armoured troop tactics. In May 1940 Giraud was captured. When he escaped two years later he made his way to Vichy France, so as to try and persuade Marshal Pétain to cease the accommodation with Germany: he was convinced that the Nazis would end by losing the war. After his views were rejected, he was secretly contacted by the Allies. He then became leader of the Free French army in Africa. Following the Casablanca Conference (1943), he shared co-leadership of the Free French forces with de Gaulle – who did not require long to outmanoeuvre him decisively.

5. The British Navy attack, also known as Operation Catapult, on the French fleet based at this (French) Algerian port on 3 July 1940. Thirteen hundred French servicemen were killed; one battleship was sunk and five others damaged. The attack was prompted by Churchill's lack of faith in Admiral Darlan's promises to him that the defeated fleet would not fall into German hands. Whilst it caused Anglo-French rancour, the US was impressed by this sign of British commitment to standing alone against Germany.

6. *L'appel du 18 Juin*, calling for French resistance to the German occupation. Although it was to assume symbolic significance its audience was limited. Many more listened to de Gaulle's further appeal, which the BBC broadcast four days later.

7. Referring to a series of civil wars that took place in France between 1648-53. The word *fronde* means 'sling', such as the Parisian mob used in smashing the windows of supporters of Cardinal Mazarin.

8. Colombey-les-Deux-Églises (Haute-Marne). In 1934 de Gaulle purchased a substantial property, 'La Boisserie', on the edge of the village. His grave in the cemetery is inscribed, 'Charles de Gaulle, 1890-1970'. At the western end of Colombey stands a forty-four-metre-high Cross of Lorraine, to commemorate his wartime role.

9. Rassemblement du peuple français (Rally of the French People) was founded by General de Gaulle in April 1947. It advocated a constitutional revision, so as to replace the IV Republic's 'régime des parties' by presidential government. It was effectively a party itself, even if de Gaulle's (unfulfilled) ambition was for a rally, allowing other parties' members to become involved. It nevertheless succeeded in attracting support not just from a, natural, right-wing constituency, but from the Left, too. After a strong showing in the 1947 municipal elections, the RPF performed credibly in the 1951 general election, but not so well as to consolidate its position within the IV Republic. The following year a significant minority of its deputies left the party. Its decline was marked by losses in the 1953 municipal elections and in September 1955 the RPF was dissolved.

10. The Geneva Conference took place between 26 April and 20 July 1954. It was principally intended to settle outstanding issues on the Korean Peninsula, and, following the First Indochina War between France and the Viet Minh, the Vietnamese situation. The Conference's final declaration called for a general election to be held within two years. It was to serve as the prompt for a unified state, but proved unacceptable to both South Vietnam and to the US.

11. The series of events which marked the transition from the IV to the V Republic began on 13 May 1958, when French generals serving in Algeria, in the face of the Independence Movement's mounting attacks, instituted an illegal 'Committee of Civil and Army Security'. Its president was the Gaullist sympathiser, General Jacques Massu. Under pressure from him, on 15 May the commander-in-chief in Algeria, General Raoul Salan declared 'Vive de Gaulle!' from the Algiers Government-General building. Throughout, de Gaulle maintained that he would only accept power from the lawfully constituted authorities. On 29 May, President Coty appealed to the General to

confer with him, regarding the creation of a Government of National Safety and Institutional Reform. On 1 June, de Gaulle became prime minister and was granted emergency powers by the National Assembly for six months. A referendum on 28 September overwhelmingly backed the new constitution. In the subsequent November general election de Gaulle and the UNR were comfortable winners. The following month 78% of an electoral college voted for him to become president; he was inaugurated in January 1959.

12. (1882-1962) President of France. The second and last holder of this office during the IV Republic.

13. *L'armée des ombres* (*Army of Shadows*) was originally a 1943 book by Joseph Kessel, loosely based on his own experience as a Resistance fighter, and then a 1969 film adaptation, directed by Jean-Pierre Melville.

14. The date of the presidential election. It was the first such election of the V Republic to be held directly and, against expectation, de Gaulle did not win an outright majority in the first round. Although comfortably defeated in the subsequent round, François Mitterrand's showing was a strong one and was one of the first warning signs that de Gaulle's popularity was now on the wane.

GEORGES POMPIDOU

1. Exams for teacher certification.

2. Student of the École normale supérieure.

3. The name of the political movement and its journal, founded in 1899 in, anti-Semitic, reaction to the Left's championing of Alfred Dreyfus. Action Française's pre-eminent ideologist was Charles Maurras. It had a substantial influence before the reality of fascism in the 1930s caused its decline. During World War II Action Française supported the Vichy regime. Its ideas retain a certain influence.

4. Rassemblement du peuple français (Rally of the French People) was founded by General de Gaulle in April 1947. It advocated a constitutional revision, so as to replace the IV Republic's 'régime des parties' by presidential government. It was effectively a party itself, even if de Gaulle's (unfulfilled) ambition was for a rally, allowing other parties' members to become involved. It nevertheless succeeded in attracting support not just from a, natural, right-wing constituency, but from the Left, too. After a strong showing in the 1947 municipal elections, the RPF performed credibly in the 1951 general election, but not so well as to consolidate its position within the IV Republic. The following year a significant minority of its deputies left the party. Its decline was marked by losses in the 1953 municipal elections, and in September 1955

the RPF was dissolved.

5. Following the 28 September 1958 referendum that approved the new, V Republic, constitution, de Gaulle authorised his followers to form a new party, the Union pour la nouvelle république (Union for the New Republic). It soon became the largest force in French politics, before losing support to the OAS (Organisation armée secrète; see also: Ho Chi Minh, note 5) when de Gaulle's Algerian strategy became clear. From then on, it became a more exclusively Gaullist party. The General though refused to be its leader; the prime minister, Michel Debré, assumed the position covertly, instead.

6. Collective term for administrative préfects.

7. École nationale d'administration.

8. (1753-1815) Marshal of France (equivalent of field marshal); Vice-constable of France; from 1796, Napoleon's chief-of-staff. He was renowned for his organisational skills and for the ability to understand and carry out the Emperor's directions to the minutest detail.

9. Jean Froissart (c.1337-1405) was a, vivid, chronicle writer, whose principal subject was the chivalric revival of the fourteenth-century. As a scholar, he attended the English and other European courts.

10. Louis de Rouvroy, Duc de Saint-Simon's (1675-1755), gossipy, *Mémoires* depict Louis XIV and Regency court life. His original writing style would later influence such writers as Tolstoy and Proust.

11. Markovic's death produced many rumours, including the existence of group sex photos in which Mme Pompidou featured.

12. The political party begun by the former minister of finance, Valéry Giscard d'Estaing, in 1966. Its full name was Fédération nationale des républicains indépendents (FNRI).

13. The Union pour la défense de la république came into being in response to *les événements* of May 1968. It was an, indirect, successor to the UNR (see also: note 5). Within months it was renamed Union des démocrates pour la république (Union of Democrats for the Republic). As such it survived until 1976, when it was superseded by Jacques Chirac's formation, the RPR (Rassemblement pour la république – Rally for the Republic), which was intended to maintain the Gaullist identity during the liberal and centrist Giscard d'Estaing's presidency.

14. Georges Pompidou died from Walendström's Macroglobulinemia. First identified in 1944, this is a (rare) cancer affecting white blood cells. The disease tends to progress slowly and periods of remission are common.

FRANÇOIS MITTERAND

1. Indicating a false title. The name originally appeared in Molière's play *Le bourgeois gentilhomme* (*The Bourgeois Gentleman*). It is the pompous Ottoman handle assumed by the character M Jourdan.

2. The name of the political movement and its journal, founded in 1899 in, anti-Semitic, reaction to the Left's championing of Alfred Dreyfus. Action Française's pre-eminent ideologist was Charles Maurras. It had a substantial influence before the reality of fascism in the 1930s caused its decline. During World War II Action Française supported the Vichy regime. Its ideas retain a certain influence.

3. (1873-1958) A Catholic thinker and politician. In 1894 Sangnier founded the liberal movement, *Le Sillon* (*The Furrow*). His aim was to bring the Church more into line with French republican trends, and to provide an alternative to anticlerical labour movements.

4. The Order of the Gallic Francisque was the coat of arms of Marshal Pétain, which came to be used as the symbol of the Vichy regime. At least two thousand five hundred people are known to have received the award, although the archive listing all of its holders was burnt at the end of World War II.

5. A Franco-Belgian industrial group founded in 1858. It is a leader both in the energy industry – electricity and gas – and in environmental waste treatment. In 2008 it merged with Gaz de France.

6. A strand of French political life evoked by Michel Rocard at the Socialist Congress of Nantes in 1977. The Second Left is historically distinct from the traditional counterpart that draws on Marxism and a Jacobin heritage, dating back to the Revolution. It emphasises the role of associations and of unions, with a membership comprising Catholic social reformers, Social Democrats and Trotskyists. It originated in 1956 in response to both the crisis the Hungarian uprising provoked within the dominant Socialist Party, and that of the IV Republic, which was caused by the movement for Algerian independence. It would then express reservations about the V Republic constitution. Other than Rocard, key figures included Alain Savary (see also: Mgr Jean-Marie Lustiger, note 4) and Pierre Mendès-France. Its positions may be seen as a precursor of Anthony Giddens' 'Third Way'.

JEAN-PAUL SARTRE

1. Student of the École normale supérieure.

2. (1885-1949) Actor, theatre manager, and director. His students included Antonin Artaud, Jean-Louis Barrault and Marcel Marceau. Following him, Sartre drew inspiration from the Greek tradition. This was plain in his first,

Dullin-directed, play *Les Mouches*, that was partly derived from the Oresteian myth.

3. Traditionally classified as that part of metaphysics dealing with the nature and essence of things – their pure being – ontology is also concerned with their grouping into hierarchies, and subdivision, according to similarities and differences.

4. Reference to *L'Être et le Néant* (*Being and Nothingness*).

RAYMOND ARON

1. Student of the École normale supérieure.

2. Le Front Populaire was the left-wing alliance of PCF (Parti communiste français), SFIO (Section française de l'Internationale ouvrière – French Section of the Workers' International) and Radical and Socialist Parties, which took power following the 1936 general election.

3. Rassemblement du peuple français (Rally of the French People) was founded by General de Gaulle in April 1947. It advocated a constitutional revision, so as to replace the IV Republic's 'régime des parties' by presidential government. It was effectively a party itself, even if de Gaulle's (unfulfilled) ambition was for a rally, allowing other parties' members to become involved. It nevertheless succeeded in attracting support not just from a, natural, right-wing constituency, but from the Left, too. After a strong showing in the 1947 municipal elections, the RPF performed credibly in the 1951 general election, but not so well as to consolidate its position within the IV Republic. The following year a significant minority of its deputies left the party. Its decline was marked by losses in the 1953 municipal elections and in September 1955 the RPF was dissolved.

MGR JEAN-MARIE LUSTIGER

1. Shorthand for the social upheaval which erupted in May that year – otherwise known as *les événements*. These were triggered by students, and were shortly joined by widespread workers' strikes. At the height of the rioting, the V Republic's overthrow appeared a distinct possibility.

2. The most visible and vociferous student leader in 1968. He was known as 'Dany le rouge' ('Danny the Red') on account of both his politics and hair.

3. The Second Vatican Council (1962-65) was called by Pope John XXIII to address relations between the Roman Catholic Church and the contemporary world. Its modernising tendency has continued to divide Catholics, some of whom question its doctrinal authority.

4. Or, the contestation of the 'Savary Bill', named after the minister of national

education (1981-84), Alain Savary. One of the bill's aims was to limit the financing of (faith-based) private schools. Lustiger was a leader of the massive demonstrations which led to the proposed legislation's discreet withdrawal by President Mitterrand.

5. Those Catholic bishops who, at the time of the Revolution, swore to uphold the Civil Constitution of the Clergy, and marked their independence from the papacy.

6. (See also: note 3.)

AYATOLLAH KHOMEINI

1. Girolamo Savanorola (1452-98) was a Dominican friar active in Renaissance Florence. He preached republican freedom and religious reform. When this republic replaced Medici rule in the city, he enforced puritanical mores. Ultimately, under torture, he recanted and was executed.

2. Louis Antoine de Saint-Just (1767-94). The youngest of the 1792 National Convention deputies, he was at the forefront of the movement calling for Louis XVI's execution. The revolution made him a close friend of Robespierre's as well as his fellow member on the Committee of Public Safety. Supervisor of the Reign of Terror, he was executed with Robespierre.

3. Khomeini was exiled in Bursa, Turkey for eleven months (1964-65), and then in the Shia city of Najaf, Iraq until 1978.

4. (1792) The first major victory for France during the revolutionary war, which prevented Prussian troops from entering Paris.

KARL LAGERFELD

1. Indicating a false title. The name originally appeared in Molière's play *Le bourgeois gentilhomme (The Bourgeois Gentleman)*. It is the pompous Ottoman handle assumed by the character M Jourdan.

2. Balthazar Picsou is the French name for the Disney character Scrooge McDuck, uncle of Donald. The richest duck in the world is an adventurer, as well as being mean.

3. Brigitte Bardot.

4. Jean-Paul Méry was a fundraiser and member of the RPR (see also: Georges Pompidou, note 13). The scandal in which he was involved centred on illegal financing of the party and the confession he recorded on an audio cassette. It became public following his death (1999), when parts, taken from a copy of the tape, were published. President Chirac was implicated, having received 5 million francs in cash from Méry (1986) and having benefited from illegal campaign funds when he was elected in 1995. The original cassette had

been handed by Méry's lawyer – who happened to be Lagerfeld's, too – to Dominique Strauss-Kahn, when the latter was finance minister. In exchange for the tape, and the safeguarding of the RPR's secret financial dealings, the minister allegedly organised a 160 million francs tax refund for Lagerfeld. He did not reveal the cassette's existence. Various legal proceedings regarding the affair have stalled.

5. Citizen Kane's enigmatic dying word is 'Rosebud'. During the course of the film it is discovered that this is the name of the sled he was riding the day before his mother sent him away. The association is one of lost innocence and happiness.

HO CHI MINH

1. Le Front Populaire was the left-wing alliance of PCF (Parti communiste français), SFIO (Section française de l'Internationale ouvrière – French Section of the Workers' International) and Radical and Socialist Parties, which took power following the 1936 general election.

2. Jules Michelet (1798-1874) was a leading French historian, who wrote *Histoire de France*. His instincts were both republican and, coinciding with the movement, romantic. He was one of the first historians to insist that history should not just be concerned with great men and institutions, but with ordinary people too. Michelet coined the term 'Renaissance' to refer to that period.

3. Philippe Leclerc de Hauteclocque (1902-47) served as a Free French general during World War II. He participated in the Battle of the Falaise Gap and went on to liberate Paris. Following the war he was commander of the CEFEO (Corps expéditionnaire en Extrême-Orient – French Far East Expeditionary Corps). His decision to negotiate with Vietnam astounded Admiral Argenlieu. Negotiations having broken down, Leclerc returned to Paris, to warn that 'anti-communism will be a useless tool unless the problem of nationalism is resolved'. He died in an airplane accident.

4. The Fontainebleau Agreements (1946) envisaged Vietnam's affiliation within the French Union. At the conference Ho Chi Minh had pressed for an independent Vietnam. The agreements' breakdown precipitated the First Indochina War.

5. Having fought in two world wars, and following command of the French land forces in South-Asia, General Raoul Salan (1899-1984) served in Algeria. He was a leader of the Officers' insurrection in May 1958, which called for General de Gaulle's return to political life. In power, de Gaulle appointed him General Inspector of the Army. This necessitated his return to

the French mainland. When de Gaulle next obliged him to take early retirement, he plotted the 21 April 1961 Generals' *putsch* in Algeria. Its failure was succeeded by the foundation of the terrorist OAS (Organisation armée secrète), with Salan as leader. The OAS aimed to disrupt the March 1962 Évian Accords, which concluded the Algerian War. Soon after Salan was captured. His death sentence was commuted to life imprisonment, and in 1968 he was amnestied. (See also: Charles de Gaulle, note 11.)

TITO

1. A North Caucasian ethnic group displaced by Russian conquest in the nineteenth-century.
2. Members of rebel bands in the Balkans, contesting the final phase of Ottoman power.
3. Between Krushchev's fall (1964) and Brezhnev's consolidation of power (1968), the Soviet Union was led by a trio consisting of the latter, Alexei Kosygin and Nikolai Podgorny.

ANDREI SAKHAROV

1. (1898-1976) Rejecting Mendelian genetics (of recessive and dominant genes), the Ukrainian biologist and agronomist developed his own pseudoscience, 'Lysenkoism', that was derived from 'Lamarckism' (the inheritance of acquired characteristics). Coming after the devastation of famine, his research into improved crop yields earned him Stalin's patronage. Lysenko's peasant background also stood him in good stead with the Marshal, particularly in his conflicts with mainstream scientists. But, once inviolate, he eventually became the target of scientific criticism. In 1964, Sakharov said: 'He is responsible for the shameful backwardness of Soviet biology and of genetics in particular ... and for the defamation, firing, arrest, even death, of many genuine scientists.' His fall from grace was soon complete.

GOLDA MEÏR

1. (1904-76) Pinhas Lavon was Israel's minister of defence in 1954, at the time of the failed covert 'Operation Susannah'. This involved Egyptian Jews, recruited by Israeli military intelligence, planting bombs inside Egyptian-, American-, and British-owned civilian targets. The intention was to blame the bombings on the Muslim Brotherhood and Egyptian communists, so as to retain Britain's troop presence on the Suez canal. Lavon denied knowledge of the affair to his prime minister, Moshe Sharett and implicated the secretary - general of the Defence Ministry, Shimon Peres instead. Sharett sided with the

latter, as well as with chief-of-staff Moshe Dayan, who testified against Lavon. The minister resigned in February 1955. He was succeeded by former prime minister, Ben-Gurion who, before long, replaced Sharett as prime minister.

GIOVANNI AGNELLI

1. The great Italian industrial and financial group, with interests in the chemical and pharmaceutical sectors, as well as energy, metallurgy, food, insurance, and publishing.
2. Built in the sixteenth-century as a papal summer palace, it is situated on the highest of Rome's seven hills, the Quirinal. It is the Italian president's official residence.
3. The elder son of Agnelli's daughter, Margherita and of Alain Elkann.

WINSTON CHURCHILL

1. The military march/song *Le Régiment de Sambre-et-Meuse* dates from directly after the 1870-71 Franco-Prussian War. It expresses strong republican sentiment.
2. The British Navy attack, also known as Operation Catapult, on the French Fleet based at this (French) Algerian port on 3 July 1940. Thirteen hundred French servicemen were killed, one battleship was sunk and five others damaged. The attack was prompted by Churchill's lack of faith in Admiral Darlan's promises to him, that the defeated fleet would not fall into German hands. Whilst it caused Anglo-French rancour, the US was impressed by this sign of British commitment to standing alone against Germany.